The Modern JavaScript Handbook

ES6+, DOM, Async, and TypeScript Explained Without Jargon

Booker Blunt

Rafael Sanders

Miguel Farmer

Boozman Richard

How to Scan a Barcode to Get a Repository

1. **Install a QR/Barcode Scanner** – Ensure you have a barcode or QR code scanner app installed on your smartphone or use a built-in scanner in **GitHub, GitLab, or Bitbucket.**

2. **Open the Scanner** – Launch the scanner app and grant necessary camera permissions.

3. **Scan the Barcode** – Align the barcode within the scanning frame. The scanner will automatically detect and process it.

4. **Follow the Link** – The scanned result will display a **URL to the repository**. Tap the link to open it in your web browser or Git client.

5. **Clone the Repository** – Use **Git clone** with the provided URL to download the repository to your local machine.

Chapter 1: Introduction to JavaScript and the Web

Overview

In the world of web development, JavaScript has become the backbone of most modern websites and applications. This dynamic, versatile programming language runs directly in web browsers and plays a central role in creating interactive, engaging, and responsive user interfaces. Whether you're interacting with social media platforms, shopping online, or just browsing the web, JavaScript is working behind the scenes to make your experience seamless and interactive.

This chapter will introduce you to JavaScript, its history, and how it functions in conjunction with HTML and CSS to build dynamic, functional websites. We will explore the evolution of JavaScript, its crucial role in modern web development, and its key components. By the end of this chapter, you should have a solid understanding of JavaScript's place in web development, as well as an overview of the essential technologies that make up the web today.

What is JavaScript and Why is it Important?

JavaScript is a high-level, interpreted programming language primarily used for building dynamic, interactive web pages. It enables websites to respond to user input, perform complex calculations, validate forms, update content dynamically, and more—all without reloading the page. Unlike HTML, which structures a webpage, or CSS, which styles it, JavaScript brings websites to life by allowing for real-time interactions.

Here's why JavaScript is essential in today's web ecosystem:

1. **Interactivity**: JavaScript enables features like form validation, drop-down menus, animations, and infinite scrolling. Without it, websites would feel static and unresponsive to users.

2. **Client-Side Execution**: JavaScript runs directly in the user's browser, which means web pages can execute actions without needing to wait for a round trip to the server. This makes websites feel faster and more efficient.

3. **Wide Adoption**: JavaScript is supported by all modern web browsers (Chrome, Firefox, Safari, Edge, etc.), making it a universal tool for web development. This cross-platform compatibility ensures your websites work on any device.

4. **Versatility**: JavaScript can be used on both the client-side (in the browser) and the server-side (using environments like

Node.js). This versatility allows developers to use the same language for both front-end and back-end development.

5. **Growing Ecosystem**: Over the years, JavaScript has grown into a powerful ecosystem with libraries (e.g., React, Angular, Vue) and frameworks (e.g., Express, Next.js) that simplify development and offer reusable solutions for complex tasks.

In summary, JavaScript is the engine that powers modern web interactivity. Without it, the internet would be a much duller and less engaging place.

JavaScript's Role in Front-End Development

In web development, **front-end development** refers to the parts of a website or application that users directly interact with. This includes everything from the layout and design to buttons, text, images, and any interactive elements.

JavaScript plays a critical role in front-end development by enabling **dynamic behavior** on websites. While HTML provides the structure and CSS dictates the appearance, JavaScript handles the logic and actions that take place on the page.

Key tasks that JavaScript performs in front-end development include:

1. **Event Handling**: JavaScript allows you to capture and respond to events like mouse clicks, keyboard inputs, form submissions, and page loading. For example, when you click a button to open a dropdown menu, JavaScript is often the behind-the-scenes action that triggers that behavior.

2. **DOM Manipulation**: The **Document Object Model (DOM)** is a hierarchical representation of a web page's structure. JavaScript allows you to manipulate the DOM, which means you can dynamically change the content of a webpage. For instance, updating a shopping cart total without refreshing the page or adding new content based on user input.

3. **Animations**: Many modern websites feature dynamic animations, such as fading elements in and out or sliding them across the screen. JavaScript allows for smooth, performance-optimized animations that make a website feel more interactive.

4. **AJAX (Asynchronous JavaScript and XML)**: One of JavaScript's most powerful capabilities is AJAX. It allows web pages to load new data without refreshing the page. For example, when you scroll down on social media and new posts appear without needing to reload the entire page, that's AJAX in action, powered by JavaScript.

5. **Frameworks and Libraries**: Modern front-end development often leverages JavaScript frameworks and libraries, such as React, Vue, or Angular, to streamline the development

13

process. These tools allow developers to build complex applications in a more organized and efficient way.

The Browser Environment

A key reason JavaScript has become so powerful is that it runs directly in web browsers. This means when a user visits a website, the browser downloads the HTML, CSS, and JavaScript files, and the JavaScript code is executed within the browser environment.

The **browser environment** consists of the following components:

1. **The Rendering Engine**: This is the component responsible for displaying the web page. It interprets HTML and CSS to render the page content. JavaScript interacts with this engine to manipulate the page after it is loaded, such as dynamically changing text, images, or layout.
2. **The JavaScript Engine**: This is the part of the browser that executes JavaScript code. Modern browsers like Chrome use engines like **V8**, while Firefox uses **SpiderMonkey**. These engines convert JavaScript code into machine-readable instructions that can be executed quickly.
3. **The Event Loop**: JavaScript uses a mechanism called the **event loop** to manage asynchronous tasks. When you interact with a webpage (click a button, hover over an image, etc.), the event loop handles the actions and ensures that

tasks run in the correct order. It makes sure that JavaScript code doesn't block other activities like UI updates or network requests.

4. **Web APIs**: Browsers also provide access to various Web APIs that JavaScript can use to interact with things like geolocation, local storage, or even the camera. These APIs provide additional functionality that JavaScript can use to enhance user experiences without relying on external libraries or server-side code.

5. **The Console**: Browsers also have a built-in JavaScript console, which developers use to write, test, and debug their code. It's an essential tool for real-time feedback and troubleshooting.

JavaScript's ability to run directly in the browser is what makes it so responsive. It allows developers to create applications that feel fast and interactive, improving user engagement and experience.

How JavaScript Interacts with HTML and CSS

While JavaScript is primarily focused on the logic and functionality of a website, it interacts heavily with both HTML and CSS, which handle structure and style, respectively.

1. **HTML (HyperText Markup Language)**: HTML provides the structure of a webpage, defining elements like headings, paragraphs, links, images, and forms. JavaScript manipulates this structure by interacting with the **DOM** (Document Object Model), which is essentially a JavaScript representation of the HTML structure.

   - For example, JavaScript can change the text content of an HTML element using `document.getElementById("elementID").innerText = "New Text"`.
   - JavaScript can also create new HTML elements dynamically, such as adding new paragraphs or images without requiring a page reload.

2. **CSS (Cascading Style Sheets)**: CSS defines how HTML elements are presented—what colors, fonts, sizes, and positions to use. JavaScript can modify these styles dynamically based on user interaction or other events.

   - JavaScript can change CSS styles by manipulating properties like `color`, `background-color`, `width`, `height`, and more.
   - For example, JavaScript can change the background color of a button when it is clicked by using `element.style.backgroundColor = "red"`.

o It can also add or remove CSS classes from elements, triggering different visual effects like showing or hiding elements.

Together, JavaScript, HTML, and CSS form the core of web development. HTML structures the content, CSS styles it, and JavaScript adds interactivity and dynamic behavior.

Summary

JavaScript is the glue that holds the interactive web together. It allows web pages to go beyond static content, making them dynamic and responsive to user actions. Whether you're building a simple form, a complex interactive map, or a full-fledged web application, JavaScript is at the heart of modern web development.

In this chapter, we introduced JavaScript, explored its role in front-end development, and looked at how it interacts with HTML and CSS to create engaging, functional websites. Understanding JavaScript's place in the web development ecosystem is the first step in becoming proficient in creating interactive web applications that users will love.

By now, you should have a solid foundation in JavaScript's role in modern web development. In the following chapters, we will dive deeper into JavaScript's syntax, advanced features, and how to use JavaScript to build real-world applications.

Chapter 2: ES6+ Syntax and Features

Overview

JavaScript has undergone significant evolution over the past few years, with ECMAScript 6 (ES6) being a major turning point. Since its release in 2015, ES6 introduced many new features that enhanced JavaScript's capabilities, readability, and performance. These features, such as `let`, `const`, arrow functions, template literals, destructuring, and more, have become the standard in modern JavaScript development.

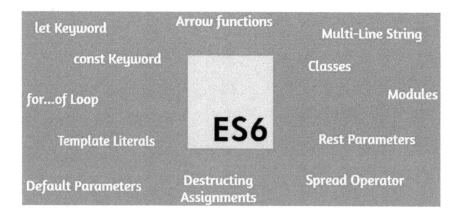

In this chapter, we'll take a deep dive into the essential updates introduced in ES6 and beyond. Understanding these new syntax features is crucial for writing efficient, clean, and modern JavaScript code. These improvements provide solutions to problems that developers had struggled with in previous versions, offering a smoother and more consistent coding experience.

By the end of this chapter, you'll be comfortable using these ES6+ features in your projects, and you'll have learned how to refactor older JavaScript code to be more modern and maintainable.

Let/const vs var

In earlier versions of JavaScript, the `var` keyword was the primary way to declare variables. However, `var` comes with several issues that make it less ideal for modern JavaScript, especially when working with block-level scopes or when needing to ensure immutability.

The Problem with `var`

Before ES6, `var` was used for variable declaration. However, `var` has function scope, which means that a variable declared with `var` is accessible throughout the function, even if it is defined inside a block (like inside an `if` statement). This can lead to unexpected behavior in certain situations.

For example:

```javascript
function example() {
    if (true) {
        var x = 10;
    }
    console.log(x); // 10, even though 'x' was
declared inside the 'if' block
}
```

Solution: `let` and `const`

ES6 introduced two new ways to declare variables: `let` and `const`.

1. **`let`**: The `let` keyword allows you to declare variables that are scoped to the block, statement, or expression in which they are defined. This solves many of the problems associated with `var` by ensuring that the variable's scope is limited to the block it's declared in.

```javascript
function example() {
    if (true) {
        let x = 10;
        console.log(x); // 10
    }
    console.log(x); // Error: x is not defined
}
```

In the example above, x is only accessible within the `if` block, and trying to access it outside of the block results in an error.

2. **const**: The `const` keyword is used to declare variables whose values cannot be reassigned. While `let` is used for variables that may change over time, `const` is used for values that should remain constant once assigned.

javascript

```
const PI = 3.14;
PI = 3.14159; // Error: Assignment to constant
variable.
```

In this case, trying to reassign the value of `PI` results in an error, making `const` an excellent choice for values that shouldn't be modified.

Arrow Functions

Arrow functions provide a shorter syntax for writing functions in JavaScript. They are particularly useful for writing concise code and preserving the context (`this`) in certain scenarios.

Traditional Function Declaration

Before ES6, a function was declared like this:

```
javascript
```

```
function add(a, b) {
    return a + b;
}
```

Arrow Function Syntax

ES6 introduced a more concise syntax for functions using arrow functions (=>):

```
javascript
```

```
const add = (a, b) => a + b;
```

The arrow function syntax makes the code more compact and easier to read, especially for simple functions.

Benefits of Arrow Functions

1. **No Binding of `this`**: One of the most useful features of arrow functions is that they do not create their own `this` context. Instead, they inherit `this` from the surrounding code. This is especially useful in callbacks and event handlers where you want to preserve the value of `this`.

```
javascript
```

```
const obj = {
```

```
    name: 'Alice',
    greet: function() {
        setTimeout(() => {
            console.log(`Hello, ${this.name}`); //
Arrow function inherits 'this' from greet()
        }, 1000);
    }
};


obj.greet(); // Outputs: Hello, Alice
```

In the above example, the arrow function inside `setTimeout`
correctly refers to the `this` context of the `greet` method, which is
`obj`.

Template Literals

Template literals offer a new way to create strings in JavaScript.
Instead of using concatenation with `+`, template literals use
backticks (`` ` ``) and allow for embedding expressions inside strings
with `${}`.

Traditional String Concatenation
```
javascript


let name = "Alice";
let greeting = "Hello, " + name + "!";
```

```
console.log(greeting); // "Hello, Alice!"
```

Template Literals

Template literals make this cleaner and more readable:

```
javascript
```

```javascript
let name = "Alice";
let greeting = `Hello, ${name}!`;
console.log(greeting); // "Hello, Alice!"
```

Multi-Line Strings

Template literals also allow for multi-line strings without needing to use escape characters (\n).

```
javascript
```

```javascript
let message = `This is a message
that spans multiple
lines.`;
console.log(message);
```

This feature is particularly useful when working with HTML templates or large text blocks in JavaScript.

Destructuring

Destructuring is a shorthand syntax that makes it easier to extract values from arrays or objects and assign them to variables.

Array Destructuring

Before ES6, extracting values from arrays was done using index-based access:

javascript

```
let arr = [1, 2, 3];
let first = arr[0];
let second = arr[1];
```

With destructuring, you can assign the values directly:

javascript

```
let [first, second] = [1, 2, 3];
console.log(first); // 1
console.log(second); // 2
```

Object Destructuring

For objects, destructuring allows you to extract properties and assign them to variables:

javascript

```
let person = { name: "Alice", age: 25 };
let { name, age } = person;
console.log(name); // Alice
console.log(age); // 25
```

You can also assign default values if the property doesn't exist:

javascript

```
let person = { name: "Alice" };
let { name, age = 30 } = person;
console.log(age); // 30 (default value)
```

Default Parameters

Default parameters allow you to specify default values for function parameters. This eliminates the need for checking if a parameter is undefined inside the function body.

javascript

```
function greet(name = "Guest") {
    console.log(`Hello, ${name}!`);
}

greet(); // Outputs: Hello, Guest!
greet("Alice"); // Outputs: Hello, Alice!
```

In the above example, the function `greet` has a default parameter of "`Guest`", so if no argument is passed, it uses the default value.

Spread/Rest Operators

The spread (. . .) and rest (. . .) operators are powerful features that allow you to work with arrays, objects, and functions more efficiently.

Spread Operator

The spread operator is used to unpack elements from an array or object, allowing you to , combine, or pass elements easily.

For arrays:

javascript

```
let arr1 = [1, 2, 3];
let arr2 = [...arr1, 4, 5];
console.log(arr2); // [1, 2, 3, 4, 5]
```

For objects:

javascript

```
let obj1 = { name: "Alice", age: 25 };
```

```
let obj2 = { ...obj1, location: "New York" };
console.log(obj2); // { name: 'Alice', age: 25,
location: 'New York' }
```

Rest Operator

The rest operator collects multiple elements into an array or object. It is typically used in function parameters or for gathering elements in an array.

For function parameters:

javascript

```
function sum(...numbers) {
    return numbers.reduce((total, num) => total +
num, 0);
}

console.log(sum(1, 2, 3, 4)); // 10
```

For objects:

javascript

```
let { name, ...otherDetails } = { name: "Alice", age:
25, location: "New York" };
console.log(otherDetails); // { age: 25, location:
'New York' }
```

Hands-On Project: Refactoring Old JavaScript Code Using ES6+ Features

In this hands-on project, you'll be refactoring an older JavaScript codebase to incorporate the new ES6+ features. We'll start with an old-style JavaScript function that uses `var`, long function syntax, and poor readability. Your goal will be to rewrite it using `let`/`const`, arrow functions, template literals, destructuring, and other ES6+ features.

Old JavaScript Code:

```javascript
function greet(name) {
    var message = "Hello, " + name + "!";
    return message;
}

function calculateTotal(price, tax) {
    var total = price + price * tax;
    return total;
}

var user = { name: "Alice", age: 25 };
```

Refactored JavaScript Code (using ES6+ features):

```javascript
```

```
const greet = (name) => `Hello, ${name}!`;

const calculateTotal = (price, tax) => price + price
* tax;

const user = { name: "Alice", age: 25 };

const { name, age } = user;

console.log(greet(name)); // Outputs: Hello, Alice!
console.log(calculateTotal(100, 0.15)); // Outputs:
115
```

In this project, you'll explore how using ES6+ features improves readability, reduces potential errors, and modernizes your codebase.

Conclusion

ES6+ brought a wealth of new features to JavaScript, many of which have become indispensable in modern web development. From `let` and `const` to arrow functions, template literals, and destructuring, these new syntax improvements make code cleaner, more efficient, and easier to maintain.

In this chapter, we explored some of the most important features of ES6 and beyond, providing you with the tools to write more modern and maintainable JavaScript code. Whether you're working on small scripts or large applications, understanding and utilizing these features will help you write better code and improve your overall development workflow.

Chapter 3: Working with the DOM (Document Object Model)

Overview

In web development, creating interactive, dynamic user interfaces is a core part of building modern websites and applications. One of the key technologies that allow developers to manipulate the web page dynamically is **JavaScript**, and specifically, its ability to interact with the **Document Object Model** (DOM).

The DOM is a structured representation of your web page in the form of a tree, where each element in your HTML is a node. Through JavaScript, you can modify this structure—whether it's changing the content of a page, modifying styles, adding or removing elements, or responding to user interactions.

In this chapter, we'll explore the core concepts of working with the DOM. You will learn how to select and manipulate DOM elements, handle events, and dynamically create or remove elements from the page. By the end of this chapter, you'll be able to confidently write JavaScript that interacts with HTML and CSS to create engaging, interactive web applications.

What is the DOM?

Before diving into the code, it's important to understand what the DOM is. The **DOM (Document Object Model)** is essentially a programmatic representation of the HTML structure of a web page. When a browser loads a page, it parses the HTML and builds this tree-like structure, which can then be accessed and manipulated using JavaScript.

For example, when you have the following HTML:

```
html
```

```html
<!DOCTYPE html>
<html>
  <head>
    <title>My Page</title>
  </head>
  <body>
    <h1>Hello, World!</h1>
    <p>Welcome to the DOM tutorial.</p>
  </body>
</html>
```

The DOM represents this HTML document as a tree, where each element (such as `<h1>`, `<p>`, `<html>`, etc.) is a node in the tree. Using JavaScript, you can interact with and modify these nodes.

Selecting DOM Elements

The first step in manipulating the DOM is selecting the elements you want to interact with. JavaScript provides several methods to select DOM elements, each with its own use cases.

1. `getElementById`

This is one of the most commonly used methods for selecting a single element by its `id`. The `getElementById` method returns a reference to the element, or `null` if no element with the specified `id` exists.

```javascript
let heading = document.getElementById("main-heading");
console.log(heading.innerText); // Outputs: Hello, World!
```

In the example above, `getElementById` selects the element with the ID `main-heading` and assigns it to the variable `heading`.

2. `getElementsByClassName`

This method allows you to select all elements that have a specific class. It returns a **live** HTMLCollection, which automatically updates if the document is modified.

```
html
```

```
<div class="box">Box 1</div>
<div class="box">Box 2</div>
<div class="box">Box 3</div>

<script>
  let boxes = document.getElementsByClassName("box");
  console.log(boxes[0].innerText); // Outputs: Box 1
</script>
```

3. getElementsByTagName

This method selects all elements of a specific tag name. It returns an HTMLCollection of elements with that tag.

```
javascript
```

```
let paragraphs = document.getElementsByTagName("p");
console.log(paragraphs[0].innerText); // Outputs:
Welcome to the DOM tutorial.
```

4. querySelector and querySelectorAll

querySelector allows you to select the first element that matches a CSS selector. querySelectorAll, on the other hand, returns all elements that match the selector, as a static **NodeList**.

```
javascript
```

```
let firstBox = document.querySelector(".box"); //
Selects the first element with class "box"
let allBoxes = document.querySelectorAll(".box"); //
Selects all elements with class "box"
```

Modifying DOM Elements

Once you've selected an element, you can modify its content, attributes, and styles. JavaScript allows you to update the text, HTML, styles, and much more.

1. Changing Content

You can modify the content of an element by updating its `innerText` or `innerHTML` property.

javascript

```
let paragraph = document.getElementById("intro");
paragraph.innerText = "This content has been
updated!";
```

Alternatively, to modify HTML content:

javascript

```
let list = document.getElementById("my-list");
list.innerHTML = "<li>New Item</li>"; // Replaces all
list items with the new one
```

2. Modifying Attributes

You can also modify the attributes of an element, such as `src`, `href`, `class`, etc., using `setAttribute()`.

javascript

```
let image = document.querySelector("img");
image.setAttribute("src", "new-image.jpg");
image.setAttribute("alt", "New Image Description");
```

To get the current value of an attribute:

javascript

```
let link = document.querySelector("a");
let href = link.getAttribute("href");
console.log(href); // Logs the href attribute of the
link
```

3. Changing Styles

To dynamically change the style of an element, you can access its `style` property. This allows you to modify individual CSS properties directly.

javascript

```
let box = document.querySelector(".box");
box.style.backgroundColor = "blue";
```

```javascript
box.style.fontSize = "20px";
```

For multiple style changes, consider adding/removing classes with `classList`:

```javascript
box.classList.add("highlight");
box.classList.remove("highlight");
box.classList.toggle("active");
```

Event Listeners and Event Handling

Event handling is one of the most important features in JavaScript. It allows your website to respond to user actions such as clicks, typing, scrolling, etc. JavaScript uses event listeners to detect these actions and respond accordingly.

1. Adding Event Listeners

Event listeners allow you to "listen" for specific events (like clicks, key presses, etc.) on an element. You can add an event listener to an element using `addEventListener()`.

```javascript
let button = document.getElementById("myButton");
button.addEventListener("click", function() {
    alert("Button clicked!");
```

```
});
```

In this example, when the button with the ID `myButton` is clicked, the event listener triggers an alert.

2. Removing Event Listeners

You can remove an event listener by using `removeEventListener()`:

```javascript
let button = document.getElementById("myButton");

function handleClick() {
    alert("Button clicked!");
}

button.addEventListener("click", handleClick);

// Later in the code
button.removeEventListener("click", handleClick);
```

3. Event Object

When an event occurs, an event object is automatically passed to the event handler function. This object contains information about the event, such as the target element and the type of event.

```javascript
```

```
button.addEventListener("click", function(event) {
    console.log(event.target); // Logs the element
that was clicked
    console.log(event.type);   // Logs the event type
(e.g., "click")
});
```

Creating and Removing Elements Dynamically

JavaScript allows you to create new elements and add them to the DOM dynamically. This can be useful when you need to add new content to the page without reloading it.

1. Creating New Elements

You can create a new element using `document.createElement()`:

javascript

```
let newDiv = document.createElement("div");
newDiv.innerText = "This is a new div!";
document.body.appendChild(newDiv); // Adds the new
div to the body
```

2. Removing Elements

To remove an element, you can use `removeChild()` or `remove()`.

javascript

```
let element =
document.getElementById("elementToRemove");
element.parentNode.removeChild(element); // Removes
the element from its parent

// Or
element.remove(); // Removes the element directly
```

3. Inserting New Elements

You can insert new elements before or after existing elements using `insertBefore()` or `insertAdjacentElement()`.

```
javascript
```

```
let existingElement =
document.querySelector(".existing");
let newElement = document.createElement("p");
newElement.innerText = "This is a newly inserted
paragraph.";

existingElement.parentNode.insertBefore(newElement,
existingElement);
```

Hands-On Project: Build an Interactive To-Do List App

Now that you understand the basics of DOM manipulation, let's put your knowledge to the test by building a simple **interactive to-do list app**.

In this project, we'll:

- Add tasks
- Remove tasks
- Mark tasks as complete
- Persist data temporarily in the browser (using `localStorage`)

Step 1: HTML Structure

```
html
```

```html
<!DOCTYPE html>
<html lang="en">
<head>
    <meta charset="UTF-8">
    <meta name="viewport" content="width=device-width, initial-scale=1.0">
    <title>To-Do List</title>
    <link rel="stylesheet" href="style.css">
</head>
<body>
```

```html
    <h1>To-Do List</h1>
    <input type="text" id="task-input"
placeholder="New Task">
    <button id="add-task">Add Task</button>
    <ul id="task-list"></ul>

    <script src="script.js"></script>
</body>
</html>
```

Step 2: JavaScript Logic
javascript

```javascript
// Selecting DOM elements
const taskInput = document.getElementById("task-input");
const addTaskButton = document.getElementById("add-task");
const taskList = document.getElementById("task-list");

// Add a task
addTaskButton.addEventListener("click", () => {
    const taskText = taskInput.value.trim();
    if (taskText !== "") {
        const newTask = document.createElement("li");
        newTask.innerText = taskText;

        // Add event listener to mark task as
complete
```

```
newTask.addEventListener("click", () => {
    newTask.classList.toggle("completed");
});

// Add event listener to remove task
newTask.addEventListener("dblclick", () => {
    taskList.removeChild(newTask);
});

taskList.appendChild(newTask);
taskInput.value = ""; // Clear the input
}
});
```

Step 3: Styling (Optional)

css

```css
/* Style the to-do list */
li.completed {
    text-decoration: line-through;
    color: gray;
}


button {
    background-color: #4CAF50;
    color: white;
    padding: 10px 15px;
    border: none;
    cursor: pointer;
}
```

```
button:hover {
    background-color: #45a049;
}

input {
    padding: 10px;
    font-size: 16px;
}
```

Conclusion

By working through this chapter, you've learned how to interact with the DOM using JavaScript. You now know how to select, modify, and create elements on the page dynamically. You also understand the importance of event handling in creating responsive web applications. This knowledge is fundamental for building interactive, user-friendly websites and applications.

Chapter 4: Asynchronous JavaScript – Callbacks, Promises, and Async/Await

Overview

Asynchronous programming is a cornerstone of modern web development, allowing JavaScript to handle tasks such as reading files, making network requests, and interacting with databases without freezing or blocking the user interface. Understanding how asynchronous code works is essential for building efficient and responsive web applications.

In this chapter, we'll explore how JavaScript handles asynchronous operations through callbacks, promises, and async/await. These concepts are critical for executing operations that take time (like fetching data from an API or reading from a file) without interrupting the normal flow of the program.

By the end of this chapter, you'll have a strong understanding of how to use these techniques to work with asynchronous JavaScript and manage tasks that run in the background while keeping your app's interface responsive.

Promise Chains	Async/Await
• Only the promise chain itself is asynchronous	• The entire wrapper function is asynchronous
Scope	
• Synchronous work can be handled in the same callback • Multiple promises use Promise.all()	• Synchronous work needs to be moved out of the callback • Multiple promises can be handled with simple variables
Logic	
• Then • Catch • Finally	• Try • Catch • Finally
Error Handling	

What is Asynchronous JavaScript?

In traditional (synchronous) JavaScript, operations are executed line by line. Each operation must finish before the next one can begin. This is fine for small tasks, but it can be problematic when dealing with operations like network requests, file I/O, or timers, which can take time.

Asynchronous programming in JavaScript allows you to run tasks that take time **in the background** while the rest of the code continues to execute. This means your application can remain responsive while these operations are happening.

For example, when you fetch data from a server, you don't want your entire web page to freeze while waiting for the response. Asynchronous programming ensures that JavaScript can continue processing other tasks while waiting for the response.

Callbacks and Callback Hell

What is a Callback?

A **callback** is a function passed into another function as an argument that is intended to be executed after some kind of event or task has finished. This is one of the most basic ways to handle asynchronous operations in JavaScript.

Here's an example of a simple callback:

```javascript
function fetchData(callback) {
    setTimeout(() => {
        let data = "Data from server";
        callback(data);
    }, 2000);
```

```
}
```

```
fetchData(function(result) {
    console.log(result); // Outputs: Data from server
after 2 seconds
});
```

In this example, the `fetchData` function simulates an asynchronous operation (like fetching data from a server). It takes a callback function that will be executed once the data is ready.

Callback Hell

While callbacks are useful, they can become difficult to manage when multiple asynchronous operations depend on each other. This creates a situation called **callback hell** or **pyramid of doom**, where you have nested callbacks inside callbacks, making the code harder to read and maintain.

For example:

```
javascript
```

```
fetchData(function(data) {
    processData(data, function(processedData) {
        saveData(processedData, function(savedData) {
            displayData(savedData);
        });
    });
```

```
});
```

In this code, the callback functions are nested within each other, creating a "pyramid" structure. This is hard to maintain and debug, and as the complexity of the operations grows, the code can become nearly impossible to follow.

Introduction to Promises

What is a Promise?

A **promise** is a more structured and elegant way to handle asynchronous operations. A promise represents the result of an asynchronous operation that may either be resolved (successful) or rejected (failed) at some point in the future.

A promise has three states:

1. **Pending**: The operation is still ongoing.
2. **Resolved**: The operation completed successfully, and a value is returned.
3. **Rejected**: The operation failed, and an error is returned.

You can create a promise using the `Promise` constructor:

```javascript
let myPromise = new Promise((resolve, reject) => {
```

```
    let success = true; // Simulate success or
failure
    if (success) {
        resolve("Operation completed successfully.");
    } else {
        reject("Operation failed.");
    }
});

myPromise
    .then((result) => {
        console.log(result); // If the promise is
resolved
    })
    .catch((error) => {
        console.log(error); // If the promise is
rejected
    });
```

In this example, `resolve` is called when the operation is successful, and `reject` is called when the operation fails. Using `.then()` and `.catch()`, you can handle the resolved value or the error in a clean, readable way.

Chaining Promises

Promises are often chained to handle multiple asynchronous operations in sequence. Each `.then()` method returns a new promise, so you can chain multiple operations together.

```javascript
javascript

fetchData()
    .then((data) => {
        return processData(data); // processData
returns a promise
    })
    .then((processedData) => {
        return saveData(processedData); // saveData
returns a promise
    })
    .then((savedData) => {
        displayData(savedData); // Final action
    })
    .catch((error) => {
        console.log("Error: ", error);
    });
```

In this example, each asynchronous operation is handled sequentially using `.then()`. If any operation fails, it will jump to the `.catch()` block, preventing the rest of the operations from running.

Working with Async/Await

What is Async/Await?

Async/await is a modern syntax introduced in ES2017 that makes working with promises more readable and easier to understand. It allows you to write asynchronous code that looks and behaves more like synchronous code.

- **async**: This keyword is used before a function to indicate that the function contains asynchronous code.
- **await**: This keyword is used inside an `async` function to pause the execution of the function until a promise is resolved.

Using `async/await`

With `async/await`, you can write asynchronous code that is easier to read and maintain, without the need for chaining `.then()` methods.

```javascript
async function fetchData() {
    let response = await fetch("https://api.example.com/data");
    let data = await response.json();
    console.log(data);
}

fetchData();
```

In this example, the `fetchData` function is marked as `async`. The `await` keyword is used to pause the execution of the function until the promise returned by `fetch()` is resolved. This eliminates the need for callbacks or chaining promises.

Error Handling with `async/await`

Error handling in `async/await` is done using `try` and `catch` blocks, which are much like how you handle errors in synchronous code.

javascript

```javascript
async function fetchData() {
    try {
        let response = await
fetch("https://api.example.com/data");
        if (!response.ok) {
            throw new Error("Network response was not
ok");
        }
        let data = await response.json();
        console.log(data);
    } catch (error) {
        console.log("Error: ", error);
    }
}

fetchData();
```

In this example, if the network request fails or the server responds with an error, the code inside the `catch` block will execute.

Error Handling in Asynchronous Code

Handling errors in asynchronous code is a crucial part of writing robust applications. JavaScript offers several ways to handle errors depending on whether you are using callbacks, promises, or async/await.

Callbacks

In callbacks, errors are typically passed as the first argument to the callback function. This is a common pattern called **error-first callback**.

```javascript
function fetchData(callback) {
    let success = false; // Simulate failure
    if (success) {
        callback(null, "Data fetched successfully.");
    } else {
        callback("Error fetching data", null);
    }
}

fetchData((error, result) => {
```

```
    if (error) {
        console.log(error); // Handle error
    } else {
        console.log(result); // Process result
    }
});
```

Promises

In promises, errors are handled using the `.catch()` method. This method will catch any error that occurs during the promise lifecycle, including those thrown by the asynchronous code inside the promise.

javascript

```
let fetchData = new Promise((resolve, reject) => {
    let success = false;
    if (success) {
        resolve("Data fetched successfully.");
    } else {
        reject("Error fetching data");
    }
});

fetchData
    .then((result) => {
        console.log(result);
    })
    .catch((error) => {
```

```
        console.log(error); // Handle error
    });
```

Async/Await

With `async/await`, errors are handled using `try/catch` blocks.
This syntax is more intuitive and looks like synchronous code,
making it easier to handle errors.

```javascript

async function fetchData() {
    try {
        let response = await
fetch("https://api.example.com/data");
        if (!response.ok) {
            throw new Error("Error fetching data");
        }
        let data = await response.json();
        console.log(data);
    } catch (error) {
        console.log(error); // Handle error
    }
}


fetchData();
```

Using `try/catch` makes error handling in asynchronous code much
cleaner and more manageable.

Hands-On Project: Create an App that Fetches Data from a Public API

In this hands-on project, we'll create a simple app that fetches data from a public API and displays it on the page. We'll use promises and async/await to handle the asynchronous nature of fetching data.

Step 1: HTML Structure

html

```html
<!DOCTYPE html>
<html lang="en">
<head>
    <meta charset="UTF-8">
    <meta name="viewport" content="width=device-width, initial-scale=1.0">
    <title>Fetch Data from API</title>
</head>
<body>
    <h1>Random User Info</h1>
    <button id="fetchData">Fetch Data</button>
    <div id="userInfo"></div>

    <script src="app.js"></script>
</body>
</html>
```

Step 2: JavaScript Logic

javascript

```
document.getElementById("fetchData").addEventListener
("click", fetchData);

async function fetchData() {
    const userInfoDiv =
document.getElementById("userInfo");
    userInfoDiv.innerHTML = "Loading...";

    try {
        let response = await
fetch("https://randomuser.me/api/");
        let data = await response.json();
        let user = data.results[0];

        userInfoDiv.innerHTML = `
            <h2>${user.name.first}
${user.name.last}</h2>
            <p>Age: ${user.dob.age}</p>
            <img src="${user.picture.medium}"
alt="User Image">
        `;
    } catch (error) {
        userInfoDiv.innerHTML = "Error fetching data:
" + error.message;
    }
}
```

Step 3: Explanation

1. We set up an event listener for the "Fetch Data" button.

2. When the button is clicked, the `fetchData` function is
   triggered.

3. The `fetchData` function uses the `fetch()` API to get data
   from the `randomuser.me` API.

4. We use `await` to wait for the response, and then parse the
   JSON data.

5. The user's name, age, and picture are displayed on the page.

6. If there's an error (e.g., network issues), it's caught in the
   `catch` block and displayed to the user.

Conclusion

This chapter has introduced the essential concepts of asynchronous
programming in JavaScript, covering **callbacks, promises**, and
async/await. Each of these techniques plays a crucial role in
handling operations that take time, such as network requests, in a
non-blocking, efficient manner.

You've learned how to manage asynchronous tasks using the various
tools JavaScript provides and have worked through a hands-on
project that fetches and displays data from a public API.
Asynchronous programming is a critical skill in web development,
and understanding how to effectively use callbacks, promises, and

async/await will help you build responsive, user-friendly applications.

Chapter 5: Object-Oriented JavaScript (OOP)

Overview

Object-Oriented Programming (OOP) is a programming paradigm that is widely used in modern software development. It organizes code around objects and data rather than functions and logic. This makes it easier to manage complex systems and allows for code that is reusable, scalable, and easier to maintain.

JavaScript, traditionally known as a functional and procedural language, also supports OOP. In this chapter, we will dive into the key principles of Object-Oriented Programming in JavaScript, including how to define and use classes, create instances, and leverage inheritance. We will also explore the concepts of encapsulation and abstraction, which help in organizing and managing complex applications.

By the end of this chapter, you will be able to understand and apply object-oriented principles to your JavaScript applications, creating well-structured, modular, and maintainable code.

What is Object-Oriented Programming?

At its core, **Object-Oriented Programming** is about organizing code into objects. Each object can have:

1. **Properties (attributes)**: These are values or data associated with the object, such as a name, age, or email.
2. **Methods (functions)**: These are actions or behaviors the object can perform, such as sending an email, updating a contact's details, or calculating a discount.

In OOP, objects are instances of **classes**, which are templates or blueprints for creating objects. The class defines the properties and methods that the objects will have.

For example, think of a **Person** class. The properties of a person might be `name`, `age`, and `email`, and the methods might include `greet()` or `updateEmail()`. When you create a **Person object**, you create an instance of the **Person class**, where the object has its own specific values for `name`, `age`, and `email`.

Key Concepts in Object-Oriented JavaScript

1. Classes and Instances

In JavaScript, a **class** is a blueprint for creating objects. It defines the properties and methods that an object created from that class will have.

- A **class** defines the structure of the object.

- An **instance** is a specific object created from a class.

Creating a Class

Here's how you can define a class in JavaScript:

javascript

```javascript
class Person {
    // Constructor method to initialize properties
    constructor(name, age) {
        this.name = name;
        this.age = age;
    }

    // Method to greet the person
    greet() {
        console.log(`Hello, my name is ${this.name}
and I am ${this.age} years old.`);
    }
}


// Creating an instance of the Person class
const person1 = new Person("Alice", 30);

// Calling the greet method
person1.greet(); // Outputs: Hello, my name is Alice
and I am 30 years old.
```

In this example:

- `Person` is the class.
- `person1` is an instance of the `Person` class.
- The `constructor()` method is a special method used to initialize new objects with values for their properties.
- `greet()` is a method that each instance of `Person` will have access to.

2. Constructors and Methods

- **Constructor:** The `constructor()` is a special function used to create and initialize an object created from a class. It is automatically called when a new instance of the class is created using the `new` keyword.
- **Methods:** Methods are functions that are defined inside a class and are available to all instances of the class. These methods can perform actions on the object's properties.

Example: Constructor and Methods
javascript

```
class Car {
    constructor(make, model, year) {
        this.make = make;
        this.model = model;
        this.year = year;
    }
```

```
    getCarInfo() {
        return `${this.year} ${this.make}
${this.model}`;
    }

    startEngine() {
        console.log("The engine is now running.");
    }
}

const car1 = new Car("Toyota", "Corolla", 2020);
console.log(car1.getCarInfo()); // Outputs: 2020
Toyota Corolla
car1.startEngine(); // Outputs: The engine is now
running.
```

In this example:

- The `constructor()` method initializes the `make`, `model`, and `year` properties for the new `Car` object.
- The `getCarInfo()` method returns a string with the car's details, and the `startEngine()` method simulates starting the car's engine.

3. Inheritance and Prototypes

One of the most powerful features of OOP is **inheritance**. Inheritance allows a class to inherit properties and methods from another class. This allows for code reuse and the creation of more specialized classes based on general ones.

- **Parent Class**: A general class that other classes can inherit from.
- **Child Class**: A class that inherits from a parent class and can override or extend its functionality.

Inheritance Example
javascript

```javascript
class Animal {
    constructor(name) {
        this.name = name;
    }

    speak() {
        console.log(`${this.name} makes a noise.`);
    }
}

class Dog extends Animal {
    constructor(name, breed) {
        super(name); // Calls the parent class
constructor
        this.breed = breed;
    }

    speak() {
```

```
        console.log(`${this.name} barks.`);
    }
}
```

```
const dog1 = new Dog("Buddy", "Golden Retriever");
dog1.speak(); // Outputs: Buddy barks.
```

In this example:

- The `Dog` class inherits from the `Animal` class using the `extends` keyword.
- The `super(name)` calls the constructor of the parent class (`Animal`) to initialize the `name` property.
- The `speak()` method is overridden in the `Dog` class, so that a `Dog` object will bark instead of just making a noise.

Prototypes and Inheritance

Every JavaScript object has a prototype. The prototype is another object that serves as a fallback for properties and methods. If a method or property isn't found on the object itself, JavaScript will look for it on the object's prototype.

This allows classes to share methods and properties without duplicating them in every instance.

4. Encapsulation and Abstraction

Encapsulation refers to bundling the data (properties) and methods that work on that data into a single unit or class. It's about restricting access to certain parts of an object to ensure the object is used only in a controlled manner.

Abstraction is the concept of hiding complex implementation details and showing only the essential features of the object. It allows you to focus on what the object does, rather than how it does it.

Encapsulation in JavaScript

Encapsulation can be achieved using **private fields** (in newer JavaScript versions) or by using closures to keep properties private.

javascript

```
class Person {
    #name; // Private field
    constructor(name, age) {
        this.#name = name;
        this.age = age;
    }

    getName() {
        return this.#name; // Accessing the private
field through a public method
```

```
    }
}
```

```
const person1 = new Person("Alice", 30);
console.log(person1.getName()); // Outputs: Alice
// console.log(person1.#name); // Error: Private
field '#name' must be declared in an enclosing class
```

In this example:

- `#name` is a **private field**. It can only be accessed from within the class, not from outside it.
- The `getName()` method is a **public method** that allows access to the private `#name` field.

Abstraction in JavaScript

Abstraction hides complex implementation details from the user. For example, if you have a `Car` class, the user doesn't need to know how the car's engine starts. They just call a `startEngine()` method, and it works.

```
javascript
```

```
class Car {
    startEngine() {
        this._ignite();
    }
```

```
    _ignite() {
        console.log("Igniting the engine...");
    }
}


const car1 = new Car();
car1.startEngine(); // Outputs: Igniting the
engine...
```

In this example:

- The `_ignite()` method is the **hidden implementation** of starting the engine, while `startEngine()` is the **public interface** that simplifies the user's experience.

Hands-On Project: Build a Simple Class-Based App (Contact Manager)

In this hands-on project, we'll create a simple **Contact Manager** app using object-oriented principles. The app will allow the user to add, view, and delete contacts.

Step 1: HTML Structure
```
html
```

```
<!DOCTYPE html>
<html lang="en">
<head>
    <meta charset="UTF-8">
```

```html
    <meta name="viewport" content="width=device-
width, initial-scale=1.0">
    <title>Contact Manager</title>
</head>
<body>
    <h1>Contact Manager</h1>
    <button id="addContact">Add Contact</button>
    <ul id="contactList"></ul>

    <script src="app.js"></script>
</body>
</html>
```

Step 2: JavaScript Logic (OOP)

```javascript
javascript

class Contact {
    constructor(name, phone) {
        this.name = name;
        this.phone = phone;
    }

    getContactInfo() {
        return `${this.name} - ${this.phone}`;
    }
}

class ContactManager {
    constructor() {
        this.contacts = [];
```

```javascript
    }

    addContact(name, phone) {
        const newContact = new Contact(name, phone);
        this.contacts.push(newContact);
    }

    displayContacts() {
        const contactList =
document.getElementById("contactList");
        contactList.innerHTML = '';
        this.contacts.forEach((contact, index) => {
            const contactItem =
document.createElement("li");
            contactItem.innerText =
contact.getContactInfo();
            contactList.appendChild(contactItem);
        });
    }
}

// Instantiate ContactManager
const manager = new ContactManager();

// Add event listener to the button
document.getElementById("addContact").addEventListene
r("click", () => {
    const name = prompt("Enter name:");
    const phone = prompt("Enter phone number:");
```

```
manager.addContact(name, phone);
manager.displayContacts();
});
```

Step 3: Explanation

1. **Contact Class**: This class defines the structure of a contact, with properties for `name` and `phone` and a method `getContactInfo()` to display the contact information.

2. **ContactManager Class**: This class manages the list of contacts. It has methods to add new contacts and display all existing contacts in the HTML page.

3. **Adding Contacts**: When the user clicks the "Add Contact" button, they are prompted to enter a name and phone number. The contact is added to the `contacts` array, and the contact list is updated.

Conclusion

In this chapter, we covered the essential principles of **Object-Oriented Programming (OOP)** in JavaScript. We explored **classes, instances, constructors, methods, inheritance, encapsulation,** and **abstraction**, all of which are key to writing modular, reusable, and maintainable code.

We also built a **contact manager** application to apply what we learned. By organizing the app into classes, we created a clear structure that is easy to extend and manage.

With a solid understanding of OOP in JavaScript, you can now create more complex applications with cleaner, more organized code.

Chapter 6: Functions and Closures

Overview

JavaScript is a function-oriented language, and understanding how functions work is essential for mastering the language. Functions are one of the core building blocks in JavaScript, and their behavior is central to writing clean, efficient, and maintainable code.

This chapter will focus on key topics such as **function declarations**, **function expressions, closures, lexical scoping, arrow functions**, **function currying**, and **function composition**. We will also look at how closures can be used to manage the state of an application through a hands-on project.

By the end of this chapter, you will have a solid understanding of how functions work in JavaScript and how to use them to create powerful, reusable code that is both flexible and maintainable.

What is a Function in JavaScript?

In programming, a **function** is a block of reusable code that performs a specific task. Functions are used to organize and structure code by breaking down complex tasks into smaller, manageable pieces. In JavaScript, functions can be declared and executed in a variety of ways.

A **function** typically consists of:

- **Parameters**: Input values that the function uses to perform its task.
- **Body**: The code that performs the task.
- **Return Value**: The result that the function produces after completing its task.

For example:

javascript

```javascript
function greet(name) {
    return `Hello, ${name}!`;
}

console.log(greet("Alice")); // Outputs: Hello, Alice!
```

In this example:

- `greet` is the function name.
- `name` is the parameter.
- The `return` statement outputs the result when the function is called.

Function Declaration vs. Function Expression

JavaScript allows you to define functions in two primary ways: **function declarations** and **function expressions**. Both have their use cases, and understanding their differences is important for writing clean and efficient JavaScript.

Function Declaration

A **function declaration** defines a named function that is available throughout the scope where it is defined. Function declarations are hoisted, meaning the function can be called before it is defined in the code.

javascript

```
// Function Declaration
function greet(name) {
    return `Hello, ${name}!`;
}
```

```
console.log(greet("Alice")); // Outputs: Hello,
Alice!
```

In this case, the `greet` function is hoisted, so you can call it anywhere in the code, even before its definition.

Function Expression

A **function expression** defines a function as part of a larger expression, typically assigned to a variable. Function expressions are **not hoisted**, meaning they can only be called after they are defined.

```javascript

// Function Expression
const greet = function(name) {
    return `Hello, ${name}!`;
};

console.log(greet("Alice")); // Outputs: Hello,
Alice!
```

In this example, the function is assigned to the `greet` variable, and it can only be invoked after the function is defined.

Key Differences

1. **Hoisting**: Function declarations are hoisted, meaning they can be called before the definition in the code. Function expressions, however, are not hoisted.
2. **Named vs. Anonymous**: Function declarations are named (e.g., `function greet() {}`). Function expressions can be either named or anonymous (e.g., `const greet = function() {}`).

Scope and Closures

What is Scope?

Scope refers to the context in which a variable is declared and accessible in your code. JavaScript has different types of scope, such as **global scope** and **local scope**.

- **Global Scope**: Variables declared outside of any function are accessible throughout the entire program.
- **Local Scope**: Variables declared within a function are only accessible within that function.

JavaScript uses **lexical scoping**, which means that the scope of a variable is determined by its position in the code at the time it is written, not when it is executed.

What is a Closure?

A **closure** is a powerful feature of JavaScript that allows functions to "remember" the environment in which they were created, even after that environment has finished executing. In other words, closures allow functions to access variables from their outer (parent) scope even after the outer function has returned.

Here's how closures work in JavaScript:

javascript

```javascript
function outerFunction() {
    let outerVar = "I am outside!";

    return function innerFunction() {
        console.log(outerVar); // innerFunction can
access outerVar
    }
}

const closureExample = outerFunction();
closureExample(); // Outputs: I am outside!
```

In this example:

- innerFunction has access to the variable outerVar even after outerFunction has finished executing. This is because of the closure.

Why are Closures Useful?

Closures are particularly useful for creating private variables or encapsulating state in JavaScript. They help prevent unwanted access to variables and allow for the creation of more modular, flexible code.

Arrow Functions and Lexical Scoping

What is an Arrow Function?

Arrow functions, introduced in ES6, provide a shorter syntax for writing functions. They are often more concise and easier to read than traditional function expressions. Arrow functions also behave differently when it comes to **lexical scoping**.

```javascript
// Traditional function
const greet = function(name) {
    return `Hello, ${name}!`;
};
```

```
// Arrow function
const greet = (name) => `Hello, ${name}!`;

console.log(greet("Alice")); // Outputs: Hello,
Alice!
```

Lexical Scoping and Arrow Functions

One of the most powerful features of arrow functions is how they handle **lexical scoping**. Unlike traditional functions, arrow functions do not have their own `this` context. Instead, they inherit `this` from the surrounding code, which makes them useful in certain scenarios, such as when working with callbacks or event handlers.

```javascript
function Timer() {
    this.seconds = 0;
    setInterval(() => {
        this.seconds++;
        console.log(this.seconds);
    }, 1000);
}

const timer = new Timer();
// Outputs the incrementing value of `seconds` every
second
```

In this example, the arrow function inside `setInterval` uses the `this` context from the `Timer` object, which is why it works as expected.

Function Currying and Composition
What is Function Currying?

Function currying is a technique in JavaScript where you transform a function that takes multiple arguments into a series of functions that each take one argument. This allows for partial application, where some arguments are fixed in advance, and the function can be called later with the remaining arguments.

javascript

```javascript
function multiply(a) {
    return function(b) {
        return a * b;
    };
}

const multiplyBy2 = multiply(2); // Partial
application
console.log(multiplyBy2(5)); // Outputs: 10
```

In this example, `multiply` is a curried function that returns another function. By calling `multiply(2)`, we create a new function `multiplyBy2`, which multiplies any given number by 2.

What is Function Composition?

Function composition is the process of combining two or more functions to produce a new function. The output of one function becomes the input for the next function in the chain.

javascript

```
const add = (x) => x + 5;
const multiply = (x) => x * 2;

const addThenMultiply = (x) => multiply(add(x));

console.log(addThenMultiply(3)); // Outputs: 16 (3 +
5 = 8, 8 * 2 = 16)
```

In this example, the `addThenMultiply` function is the composition of the `add` and `multiply` functions. It first adds 5 to the input and then multiplies the result by 2.

Hands-On Project: Create a Simple Calculator Using Closures

In this hands-on project, we'll create a simple calculator that uses closures to manage its state. The calculator will allow the user to perform basic operations like addition, subtraction, multiplication, and division.

Step 1: JavaScript Logic

javascript

```javascript
function createCalculator() {
    let result = 0; // Private variable to hold the
result

    return {
        add: function(num) {
            result += num;
            console.log(result);
        },
        subtract: function(num) {
            result -= num;
            console.log(result);
        },
        multiply: function(num) {
            result *= num;
            console.log(result);
        },
        divide: function(num) {
```

```
            if (num !== 0) {
                result /= num;
                console.log(result);
            } else {
                console.log("Cannot divide by
zero!");
            }
        },
        getResult: function() {
            return result;
        }
    };
}


const calculator = createCalculator();
calculator.add(10); // Outputs: 10
calculator.multiply(2); // Outputs: 20
calculator.subtract(5); // Outputs: 15
calculator.divide(3); // Outputs: 5
calculator.getResult(); // Returns: 5
```

Step 2: Explanation

In this project:

1. **Closure:** The `createCalculator` function returns an object
   with methods for performing operations. The `result` variable
   is encapsulated inside the closure, making it private and
   inaccessible from outside the function.

2. **State Management**: Each method (`add`, `subtract`, `multiply`, `divide`) modifies the `result` and provides feedback to the user.
3. **Flexibility**: By using closures, the calculator maintains its state between function calls, and the user can interact with it by calling its methods.

Conclusion

In this chapter, we've covered essential concepts around **functions** and **closures** in JavaScript. We explored how to define functions using both function declarations and function expressions, and we dived into closures, which allow functions to remember their lexical environment even after they've finished executing. We also covered **arrow functions, function currying**, and **function composition**, which help write clean and reusable code.

Through the **calculator project**, we saw how closures can be used to encapsulate state and make our applications more modular and flexible.

By mastering functions and closures, you can handle complex operations and state management in your JavaScript applications with ease, creating more maintainable and scalable code.

Chapter 7: Error Handling and Debugging

Overview

Every programmer, regardless of experience, encounters bugs and errors in their code. The ability to handle errors effectively and debug code systematically is a critical skill in any developer's toolbox. JavaScript, like other programming languages, has built-in mechanisms for managing errors and debugging. By learning how to handle errors and use debugging tools, you'll be able to write more robust, reliable, and maintainable code.

In this chapter, we'll explore the fundamentals of error handling in JavaScript, including how to use `try/catch` blocks to manage exceptions, how to throw custom errors, and how to debug JavaScript code effectively using browser tools like the console and breakpoints. We'll also identify common JavaScript bugs and learn how to avoid them. To reinforce these concepts, you'll complete a hands-on project that intentionally throws errors to practice debugging.

Error Handling in JavaScript

What is Error Handling?

Error handling refers to the process of anticipating, detecting, and responding to errors or exceptional conditions in your program. Errors are often unexpected, but by managing them effectively, you can prevent your application from crashing and ensure that it behaves predictably, even when something goes wrong.

In JavaScript, errors are typically handled using `try/catch` blocks, which allow you to "catch" errors when they occur and decide how to respond. Error handling helps you control what happens when something goes wrong, providing a way to either fix the issue or display an informative message to the user.

Try/Catch Blocks

The `try/catch` statement is the primary way to handle errors in JavaScript. It allows you to test a block of code for errors (in the `try` block) and catch any exceptions that occur (in the `catch` block).

Basic Syntax of Try/Catch

javascript

```
try {
    // Code that may throw an error
    let result = riskyOperation();
```

```
} catch (error) {
    // Code that handles the error
    console.log("An error occurred:", error.message);
}
```

- The code inside the `try` block is executed.
- If an error occurs, the `catch` block is executed, and the error is passed as an argument (often named `error` or `err`).

Example: Basic Try/Catch

javascript

```
try {
    let num = 10;
    let result = num / 0; // This will result in
Infinity, but no error is thrown
    console.log(result);
} catch (error) {
    console.log("Caught an error:", error.message);
// This will not be executed
}
```

In this example:

- Division by zero in JavaScript doesn't throw an error but returns `Infinity`. Thus, no error is caught by the `catch` block.

Catching Specific Errors

You can catch specific types of errors using `try/catch` blocks. If you throw an error, you can catch and handle it appropriately.

```javascript
try {
    let user = JSON.parse('invalid JSON'); // This
will throw a SyntaxError
} catch (error) {
    if (error instanceof SyntaxError) {
        console.log("There was a syntax error while
parsing JSON.");
    } else {
        console.log("An unexpected error occurred.");
    }
}
```

In this case, we check if the error is an instance of `SyntaxError` and respond accordingly.

Throwing Custom Errors

In addition to catching built-in errors, JavaScript allows you to **throw your own errors** using the `throw` keyword. This is useful for creating custom error conditions when something goes wrong in your application.

Syntax of Throwing Errors

```javascript
throw new Error("Something went wrong!");
```

You can also throw custom error types for more specific cases:

```javascript
function validateAge(age) {
    if (age < 18) {
        throw new Error("Age must be 18 or older.");
    }
    return true;
}

try {
    validateAge(16);
} catch (error) {
    console.log(error.message); // Outputs: Age must be 18 or older.
}
```

Custom Error Classes

For more complex applications, you may want to define your own error classes. This allows you to create specialized errors that can carry additional information.

```javascript
```

```
class ValidationError extends Error {
    constructor(message) {
        super(message);
        this.name = "ValidationError"; // Customize
error name
    }
}

try {
    throw new ValidationError("Invalid input.");
} catch (error) {
    console.log(`${error.name}: ${error.message}`);
// Outputs: ValidationError: Invalid input.
}
```

In this example, `ValidationError` is a custom error class that extends the built-in `Error` class. It adds a custom name and message to the error, making it more descriptive and useful for debugging.

Debugging JavaScript Code

Effective debugging is essential for identifying and fixing issues in your code. JavaScript provides a variety of tools for debugging code, including the browser's built-in **Developer Tools** (DevTools), which allow you to inspect the state of your application, set breakpoints, and interact with the execution flow.

Using the Console for Debugging

One of the simplest and most effective tools for debugging is the **console**. You can use `console.log()` to print messages, variables, and error information to the console, helping you track the flow of your code and identify problems.

javascript

```
function add(a, b) {
    console.log("Adding:", a, b); // Debugging output
    return a + b;
}

add(5, 10);
```

You can also use other console methods for debugging:

- `console.info()` – Provides general information
- `console.warn()` – Displays a warning message
- `console.error()` – Displays an error message

javascript

```
console.warn("This is a warning message.");
console.error("This is an error message.");
```

Using Breakpoints in Browser DevTools

In modern browsers, you can set **breakpoints** in your code using DevTools. Breakpoints allow you to pause the execution of your code at a specific line, inspect variables, and step through the code line by line to understand its behavior.

Here's how you can set breakpoints:

1. Open DevTools (usually by pressing F12 or right-clicking and selecting "Inspect").
2. Go to the **Sources** tab and navigate to the script you want to debug.
3. Click on the line number where you want to set the breakpoint.
4. Reload the page or trigger the function, and the code will pause at the breakpoint.
5. Use the DevTools interface to step through the code and inspect variables.

Using debugger Keyword

The `debugger` statement can be inserted directly into your code to create a breakpoint. When the code reaches this point, it will pause, and the debugger will be triggered if DevTools is open.

```javascript
```

```
function calculateDiscount(price) {
    let discount = price * 0.1;
    debugger; // Code will pause here when DevTools
are open
    return price - discount;
}


calculateDiscount(100);
```

Common JavaScript Bugs and How to Avoid Them

Understanding common JavaScript bugs is an important part of writing robust code. Here are some of the most frequent issues developers encounter and how to avoid them.

1. Undefined Variables

Accessing an undefined variable leads to runtime errors. Always initialize variables before using them.

```
javascript


let result;
console.log(result); // Undefined, but no error
```

To avoid this, ensure all variables are initialized properly before accessing them.

2. NaN (Not a Number) Issues

Attempting to perform mathematical operations with non-numeric values results in `NaN`, which can be difficult to debug.

javascript

```javascript
let result = "Hello" - 5; // NaN
console.log(result); // Outputs: NaN
```

To prevent this, check that the values involved in arithmetic operations are numbers.

javascript

```javascript
let num = parseInt("42");
if (isNaN(num)) {
    console.log("Not a valid number.");
}
```

3. Infinite Loops

Accidentally creating infinite loops can freeze or crash your program. Always ensure that loops have proper exit conditions.

javascript

```javascript
let i = 0;
while (i < 10) {
    console.log(i);
```

```
    // Missing i++ or exit condition, this will loop
infinitely
}
```

Make sure that loops have valid termination conditions.

Hands-On Project: Create an App That Intentionally Throws Errors

In this project, you'll create a simple app that intentionally throws errors so that you can practice using debugging techniques to identify and fix them.

Step 1: HTML Structure
```
html
```

```html
<!DOCTYPE html>
<html lang="en">
<head>
    <meta charset="UTF-8">
    <meta name="viewport" content="width=device-
width, initial-scale=1.0">
    <title>Error Handling and Debugging</title>
</head>
<body>
    <h1>Error Handling and Debugging Demo</h1>
    <button id="triggerError">Trigger Error</button>
    <div id="errorMessage"></div>
```

```
    <script src="app.js"></script>
</body>
</html>
```

Step 2: JavaScript Logic

```javascript
document.getElementById("triggerError").addEventListener("click", function() {
    try {
        throw new Error("This is a custom error.");
    } catch (error) {
        console.error("Caught an error:", error.message);

document.getElementById("errorMessage").textContent = error.message;
    }
});
```

Step 3: Explanation

In this project:

- We create a button that triggers an intentional error when clicked.
- Inside the `try` block, we throw a custom error.
- The `catch` block catches the error and logs it to the console, while also displaying the error message in the HTML page.

By intentionally throwing errors, you can practice debugging using the `console.log()`, `console.error()`, and other debugging tools.

Conclusion

In this chapter, we've covered the essentials of **error handling** and **debugging** in JavaScript. You've learned how to manage errors with `try/catch` blocks, how to throw custom errors, and how to debug your code using browser tools like the console and breakpoints. We also discussed common JavaScript bugs and how to avoid them.

The hands-on project helped you practice debugging techniques in a controlled environment by intentionally throwing errors. By understanding and applying these error-handling and debugging techniques, you'll be better equipped to write more robust and maintainable JavaScript code.

As you move forward, the ability to effectively handle errors and debug your code will be invaluable in creating applications that are resilient, user-friendly, and reliable.

Chapter 8: Working with APIs (Application Programming Interfaces)

Overview

In modern web development, **APIs (Application Programming Interfaces)** are integral to building dynamic and feature-rich applications. APIs allow your application to interact with external services, such as fetching data from remote servers, sending user data, or even integrating with third-party platforms.

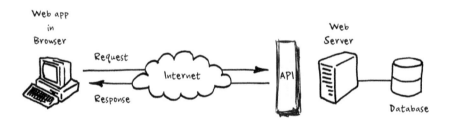

In this chapter, we will learn how to interact with APIs using JavaScript. We'll explore key topics such as making requests using the **Fetch API** and **XMLHttpRequest**, handling **JSON** responses, managing **API authentication** (such as with API keys or OAuth), dealing with **rate limiting**, and handling errors. Finally, we'll apply these concepts in a hands-on project, where we will build an app that fetches and displays weather data from a public API.

What is an API?

An **API (Application Programming Interface)** is a set of rules and protocols that allow different software applications to communicate with each other. APIs allow you to request data from an external service or send data to it. For instance, when you check the weather on your phone, the weather app is likely fetching that data from a weather API.

APIs enable developers to integrate different functionalities into their apps without needing to build everything from scratch. Instead, developers can interact with existing services (like databases, payment systems, or social media platforms) using APIs.

Fetching Data with the Fetch API and XMLHttpRequest

JavaScript provides multiple ways to send HTTP requests to external APIs and retrieve data. The two most common methods are the **Fetch API** and **XMLHttpRequest**. Let's look at both.

1. Fetch API

The **Fetch API** is a modern, promise-based way to make HTTP requests in JavaScript. It provides a more powerful and flexible feature set than the older **XMLHttpRequest**.

Basic Fetch Example
```javascript
fetch('https://api.example.com/data')
    .then(response => response.json())   // Convert
response to JSON
    .then(data => console.log(data))     // Use the data
from the API
    .catch(error => console.log('Error:', error)); //
Handle errors
```

In this example:

- `fetch()` initiates a request to the API endpoint.
- `.then(response => response.json())` processes the response and converts it into a JSON format.
- `.then(data => console.log(data))` logs the data to the console.
- `.catch()` handles any errors that might occur during the request.

Handling HTTP Status Codes

When interacting with APIs, you also need to handle different **HTTP status codes** (like 200 for success, 404 for not found, etc.). The Fetch API does not throw an error for HTTP errors by default, so you need to check the `response.ok` property.

javascript

```javascript
fetch('https://api.example.com/data')
  .then(response => {
    if (!response.ok) {
      throw new Error('Network response was not ok');
    }
    return response.json();
  })
  .then(data => console.log(data))
  .catch(error => console.log('Error:', error));
```

This way, we handle cases where the API may return an error status like 404 or 500.

2. XMLHttpRequest

Before the Fetch API, **XMLHttpRequest** was used to interact with APIs in JavaScript. Although **Fetch** is more modern and flexible, it's still important to understand **XMLHttpRequest**, especially when working with legacy code.

Basic XMLHttpRequest Example
javascript

```
var xhr = new XMLHttpRequest();
xhr.open('GET', 'https://api.example.com/data',
true);
xhr.onload = function() {
  if (xhr.status === 200) {
    console.log(JSON.parse(xhr.responseText));   //
Process the response
  } else {
    console.log('Error:', xhr.statusText);   // Handle
error
  }
};
xhr.onerror = function() {
  console.log('Network error');   // Handle network
errors
};
xhr.send();
```

In this example:

- `xhr.open('GET', url, true)` opens a new request.
- `xhr.onload` is the callback function executed when the request completes.
- `xhr.status` checks for the status code, and `xhr.responseText` contains the response data.

While XMLHttpRequest is still widely used, the Fetch API is generally preferred due to its simpler and more readable syntax, as well as its promise-based handling of asynchronous code.

Handling JSON Responses

Most APIs return data in **JSON (JavaScript Object Notation)** format, which is a lightweight data-interchange format that's easy to read and write. JavaScript has built-in methods to handle JSON, such as JSON.parse() for parsing JSON strings and JSON.stringify() for converting JavaScript objects into JSON format.

Working with JSON

Here's how to handle JSON data returned by an API:

javascript

```
fetch('https://api.example.com/data')
  .then(response => response.json())  // Parse the
JSON response
  .then(data => {
    console.log(data);  // Use the data in your
application
  })
  .catch(error => console.log('Error:', error));
```

Sending JSON Data to an API

When making a POST request, you can send data to an API in JSON format by using `JSON.stringify()` to convert your data into a JSON string.

```javascript
const postData = {
  name: 'John',
  age: 30
};

fetch('https://api.example.com/data', {
  method: 'POST',
  headers: {
    'Content-Type': 'application/json'
  },
  body: JSON.stringify(postData)
})
  .then(response => response.json())
  .then(data => console.log(data))
  .catch(error => console.log('Error:', error));
```

API Authentication (e.g., API Keys, OAuth)

Many APIs require some form of authentication to ensure that only authorized users can access the data. Two common methods of authentication are **API keys** and **OAuth.**

1. API Keys

An **API key** is a unique identifier that is passed in the request to authenticate the client making the request. It is often included in the request header or query parameters.

```javascript
const apiKey = 'your-api-key-here';

fetch(`https://api.example.com/data?api_key=${apiKey}`)
  .then(response => response.json())
  .then(data => console.log(data))
  .catch(error => console.log('Error:', error));
```

2. OAuth

OAuth is a more secure and flexible method of authentication, often used for accessing third-party services like Google, Facebook, or GitHub. OAuth involves obtaining a token from the service provider after the user has authorized the application to access their data.

Here's a simplified flow of how OAuth works:

1. The user is redirected to the service provider's authorization page.
2. The user authorizes the application to access their data.

3. The service provider returns an **access token** that the application can use to make API requests on behalf of the user.

Handling OAuth is more complex, so many developers use libraries like **OAuth.js** or **Axios** to manage the process.

Rate Limiting and Handling Errors in API Calls

What is Rate Limiting?

Rate limiting is a technique used by APIs to control the number of requests a user or application can make within a certain time period. This prevents overload on the server and ensures fair usage. When an API is rate-limited, it will return a status code (usually `429 Too Many Requests`) when the limit is exceeded.

Handling Rate Limiting

You can handle rate-limiting by checking the response headers. Most APIs return a `X-RateLimit-Remaining` header, which tells you how many requests you have left.

```javascript
fetch('https://api.example.com/data')
  .then(response => {
    if (response.status === 429) {
```

```
        console.log('Rate limit exceeded, please try
again later.');
    } else {
      return response.json();
    }
  })
  .then(data => console.log(data))
  .catch(error => console.log('Error:', error));
```

Handling API Errors Gracefully

It's essential to handle errors when making API requests, such as:

- **Network errors** (e.g., no internet connection).
- **Timeouts** (when the request takes too long).
- **Invalid responses** (e.g., 404 or 500 errors).

Using a combination of `try/catch` blocks and `.catch()` in promise chains will help ensure your application handles errors gracefully.

Hands-On Project: Fetch Weather Data from an Open API

In this hands-on project, we will build a weather app that fetches data from a public weather API and dynamically displays the weather information.

Step 1: Choose an API

We'll use the **OpenWeatherMap** API, which provides free weather data. You'll need to sign up and get an API key from OpenWeatherMap.

Step 2: HTML Structure
html

```
<!DOCTYPE html>
<html lang="en">
<head>
    <meta charset="UTF-8">
    <meta name="viewport" content="width=device-
width, initial-scale=1.0">
    <title>Weather App</title>
</head>
<body>
    <h1>Weather App</h1>
    <input type="text" id="city" placeholder="Enter
city">
    <button id="getWeather">Get Weather</button>
    <div id="weatherResult"></div>

    <script src="app.js"></script>
</body>
</html>
```

Step 3: JavaScript Logic

javascript

```javascript
document.getElementById("getWeather").addEventListene
r("click", fetchWeather);

function fetchWeather() {
    const city =
document.getElementById("city").value;
    const apiKey = 'your-api-key-here'; // Replace
with your OpenWeatherMap API key
    const url =
`https://api.openweathermap.org/data/2.5/weather?q=${
city}&appid=${apiKey}&units=metric`;

    fetch(url)
        .then(response => {
            if (!response.ok) {
                throw new Error('City not found or
API limit exceeded');
            }
            return response.json();
        })
        .then(data => {
            const weather = `
                <h2>${data.name},
${data.sys.country}</h2>
                <p>Temperature:
${data.main.temp}°C</p>
```

```
        <p>Weather:
${data.weather[0].description}</p>
        <p>Humidity:
${data.main.humidity}%</p>
        `;

document.getElementById("weatherResult").innerHTML =
weather;
        })
        .catch(error => {

document.getElementById("weatherResult").innerHTML =
`<p>Error: ${error.message}</p>`;
        });
}
```

Step 4: Explanation

1. The user inputs a city name and clicks the "Get Weather" button.

2. The `fetchWeather` function makes a GET request to the OpenWeatherMap API, including the city and the API key.

3. The response is processed and converted into JSON format.

4. The weather data is displayed dynamically on the page, showing the city name, temperature, weather description, and humidity.

5. If an error occurs (e.g., invalid city name), an error message is displayed.

Conclusion

In this chapter, you learned how to interact with external APIs in JavaScript, including how to make HTTP requests using the **Fetch API** and **XMLHttpRequest**, handle JSON responses, manage **API authentication**, and work with **rate limiting** and error handling. Through the hands-on weather app project, you practiced fetching data from an external API and displaying it dynamically on the page.

Working with APIs is a crucial skill in modern web development, and the ability to fetch, handle, and display data from external sources will help you create more interactive and data-driven web applications.

As you continue to build your applications, you'll encounter more complex use cases of APIs. Mastering these techniques will give you the foundation to work with any API, whether it's for social media, weather, finance, or other data-rich services.

Chapter 9: JavaScript Modules – Organizing Code

Overview

As JavaScript applications grow in size and complexity, organizing code effectively becomes crucial for maintaining readability, scalability, and ease of maintenance. One of the most powerful tools for organizing code in modern JavaScript is **modules**. Modules allow developers to break down a large codebase into smaller, reusable pieces that can be easily maintained, updated, and tested.

In this chapter, we'll dive into the concepts of **JavaScript modules** and how to use them for organizing your code. You will learn how to use **import/export statements**, how to structure your modules with **default and named exports**, and how to work with modules in both **Node.js** and the **browser**. Finally, we'll go through best practices for organizing a large JavaScript codebase.

By the end of this chapter, you will have a solid understanding of how to modularize your JavaScript applications, making them more maintainable, scalable, and easier to navigate.

What Are JavaScript Modules?

In JavaScript, a **module** is simply a file that contains reusable code. By splitting your application into multiple files, each handling a specific piece of functionality, you can create a more organized codebase. This modular approach is particularly useful for managing complex projects with many dependencies.

JavaScript modules allow you to:

- **Encapsulate functionality**: Keep related functionality together.
- **Avoid global namespace pollution**: Prevent variables from clashing by keeping them scoped to the module.
- **Reuse code**: Use the same code in different parts of your application without duplicating it.

Modules in JavaScript are supported natively in modern browsers and Node.js environments. They enable a clean separation of concerns and allow you to better structure your code for easier development and maintenance.

Import/Export Statements

To work with JavaScript modules, you need to understand how to **import** and **export** code between different files. This is done using the `import` and `export` statements.

Exporting Code from a Module

In order to use a function, variable, or class from one module in another, you first need to **export** it. JavaScript provides two main ways to export code: **named exports** and **default exports**.

Named Exports

With **named exports**, you can export multiple values from a module, each with its own name. Here's how it works:

javascript

```
// math.js (module)
export const add = (a, b) => a + b;
export const subtract = (a, b) => a - b;
```

In this example, we're exporting two functions, add and subtract, using the export keyword. These functions can now be imported by other modules using their names.

Default Exports

A module can also have a **default export**, which allows you to export a single value as the "default" export. This is useful when a module is focused on a single piece of functionality.

javascript

```
// calculator.js (module)
const multiply = (a, b) => a * b;
export default multiply;
```

In this case, the `multiply` function is the default export of the `calculator.js` module. You can only have one default export per module.

Importing Code from a Module

Once you've exported values from a module, you can **import** them into another file. There are two main ways to import code: **named imports** and **default imports**.

Named Imports

If you exported named functions or variables, you can import them using their exact names.

```
javascript
```

```javascript
// app.js
import { add, subtract } from './math.js';

console.log(add(2, 3)); // Outputs: 5
console.log(subtract(5, 3)); // Outputs: 2
```

In this case, we are importing the `add` and `subtract` functions from the `math.js` module. You need to match the names of the exported functions or variables exactly.

Default Imports

To import the default export from a module, you can choose any name for the imported value.

```
javascript
```

```javascript
// app.js
import multiply from './calculator.js';

console.log(multiply(2, 3)); // Outputs: 6
```

In this example, we import the default export from `calculator.js` and call it `multiply`.

Using Modules in Node.js and Browsers

JavaScript modules work slightly differently in **Node.js** and the **browser** environment, but the underlying concepts are the same.

Using Modules in Node.js

Node.js has native support for modules starting with version 12, though it uses the CommonJS module system by default. However, starting with ES6, Node.js also supports **ECMAScript modules** (ES modules). To use ES modules in Node.js, you need to either:

1. Use `.mjs` file extensions for your module files.
2. Enable ES module support by setting `"type": "module"` in your `package.json`.

Example in Node.js
```javascript
// math.mjs
export const add = (a, b) => a + b;

// app.mjs
import { add } from './math.mjs';
console.log(add(2, 3)); // Outputs: 5
```

Node.js supports the `import` and `export` syntax, just like modern browsers.

Using Modules in Browsers

In browsers, you can use **ES modules** directly by including the `type="module"` attribute in your `<script>` tag.

```html
<!-- index.html -->
<script type="module" src="app.js"></script>
```

This will tell the browser to treat `app.js` as a module, enabling the use of `import` and `export` statements.

```javascript
// app.js
import { add } from './math.js';
console.log(add(2, 3)); // Outputs: 5
```

Modules in the browser run in strict mode by default, meaning you get a more predictable and error-free environment.

Best Practices for Organizing Large JavaScript Codebases

When working with large JavaScript codebases, organizing your modules and ensuring the application's structure remains maintainable is key. Here are some best practices for working with modules:

1. Keep Your Modules Small and Focused

Each module should have a single responsibility. Avoid making large, monolithic modules that do too many things. Instead, break down the functionality into smaller, manageable pieces. For example:

- `math.js`: Contains basic math operations like addition, subtraction, etc.

- `api.js`: Handles API requests.
- `ui.js`: Handles UI interactions.

2. Use Clear Naming Conventions

Give your modules and their exported functions meaningful and consistent names. This will make it easier for other developers (or your future self) to understand the purpose of each module and function.

- `getUserData.js`: A module that fetches user data from an API.
- `parseData.js`: A module that parses raw data.

3. Avoid Circular Dependencies

Circular dependencies occur when two or more modules depend on each other, either directly or indirectly. This can create unexpected behavior and lead to issues in your application. Try to structure your modules to avoid circular dependencies by keeping them loosely coupled.

4. Use an `index.js` File to Aggregate Exports

In larger projects, you may want to aggregate exports from multiple files into a single entry point. This helps reduce the complexity of import statements in other parts of your application.

```javascript
// math/index.js
export { add } from './add.js';
export { subtract } from './subtract.js';

// app.js
import { add, subtract } from './math';
```

This pattern allows you to consolidate multiple files into a single module, making your imports cleaner and more manageable.

Hands-On Project: Build a Simple Module-Based Application

In this project, we'll build a simple **contact manager** application that's broken into multiple modules. This app will allow users to add contacts, display them, and delete them.

Step 1: Create the Contact Module

```javascript
// contact.js
export const createContact = (name, phone) => {
    return { name, phone };
};

export const displayContact = (contact) => {
```

```javascript
    console.log(`${contact.name} -
${contact.phone}`);
};
```

Step 2: Create the Contact Manager Module
javascript

```javascript
// contactManager.js
import { createContact, displayContact } from
'./contact.js';

let contacts = [];

export const addContact = (name, phone) => {
    const newContact = createContact(name, phone);
    contacts.push(newContact);
};

export const showContacts = () => {
    contacts.forEach(contact =>
displayContact(contact));
};
```

Step 3: Create the Main Application
javascript

```javascript
// app.js
import { addContact, showContacts } from
'./contactManager.js';

addContact('Alice', '123-456-7890');
```

```
addContact('Bob', '987-654-3210');
showContacts();
```

Step 4: Explanation

- `contact.js`: Contains functions to create and display individual contacts.
- `contactManager.js`: Handles the management of contacts (adding and displaying).
- `app.js`: The main entry point that ties everything together by calling the functions to add and show contacts.

In this modular app:

- Each part of the app (creating contacts, managing them, displaying them) is contained in its own module.
- This structure is scalable, meaning you can easily add more features (e.g., deleting contacts, editing them) without disrupting the existing codebase.

Conclusion

In this chapter, we've explored the concept of **JavaScript modules** and how they can help organize and scale your applications. We learned about **import/export statements, default and named exports**, and how to use modules in both **Node.js** and **browsers**. We also discussed best practices for organizing large JavaScript codebases, such as keeping modules small and focused, using clear naming conventions, and avoiding circular dependencies.

Through the **contact manager** project, we practiced modularizing code by breaking it into smaller, reusable pieces. This modular approach makes your codebase more maintainable, scalable, and easier to navigate.

By applying these module-based principles, you'll be able to build more robust applications that are easier to maintain, test, and extend in the future. As your projects grow in complexity, the organization of your code will become increasingly important, and mastering modules will be a crucial step in your development journey.

Chapter 10: TypeScript – The Supercharged JavaScript

Overview

JavaScript is a versatile and widely-used programming language, but it lacks some features that help ensure code quality and readability in larger, more complex applications. TypeScript, on the other hand, is a **superset of JavaScript** that introduces static typing, which adds type annotations to JavaScript's dynamic typing system. This powerful addition brings many benefits to developers, such as improved code quality, better tooling, and enhanced collaboration between team members.

In this chapter, we will explore **TypeScript**—what it is, how it works, and how it can be used to improve the development process. We will cover the basics of **type annotations** and **type inference**, dive into how to work with **interfaces** and **types**, explore the concepts of **classes and inheritance in TypeScript**, and demonstrate how to integrate TypeScript into existing JavaScript projects.

By the end of this chapter, you'll be equipped with the knowledge to start using TypeScript in your projects, allowing you to write cleaner, more reliable, and maintainable code.

What is TypeScript?

TypeScript is a **typed superset of JavaScript** developed by Microsoft. This means that TypeScript adds new features to JavaScript, specifically **static types**, but is still fully compatible with existing JavaScript code. TypeScript's most significant feature is its ability to add types to variables, function parameters, and return values, helping to catch errors early in the development process. It compiles down to **plain JavaScript** so that it can run in any JavaScript environment (browsers, Node.js, etc.).

TypeScript brings several advantages:

1. **Static Type Checking**: Helps catch errors early in the development cycle.
2. **Improved Tooling**: Offers better autocompletion, navigation, and refactoring support in IDEs and editors.
3. **Scalability**: Helps manage larger codebases by enforcing type safety and encouraging better code organization.
4. **Familiarity with JavaScript**: TypeScript is still JavaScript, so learning TypeScript is easy for JavaScript developers.

Key Topics in TypeScript

1. Type Annotations and Type Inference

One of the key features of TypeScript is **static typing**, which allows you to specify the types of variables, function parameters, and return values. You can do this using **type annotations**.

Type Annotations

A **type annotation** explicitly defines what type a variable, parameter, or return value should be.

typescript

```
let name: string = "John"; // name is explicitly
typed as a string
let age: number = 30; // age is explicitly typed as a
number
let isActive: boolean = true; // isActive is
explicitly typed as a boolean
```

In the example above:

- `name` is declared as a string.
- `age` is declared as a number.
- `isActive` is declared as a boolean.

By adding these type annotations, TypeScript can check if you are using the correct data type in your program. If you try to assign a value of the wrong type, TypeScript will throw an error:

typescript

```
let name: string = "John";
name = 42; // Error: Type 'number' is not assignable
to type 'string'.
```

Type Inference

TypeScript also uses **type inference**, which means it automatically determines the type of a variable based on its value when no explicit type is provided.

typescript

```
let name = "John"; // TypeScript infers 'name' to be
of type string
let age = 30; // TypeScript infers 'age' to be of
type number
```

In these examples, TypeScript infers that name is a string and age is a number based on the values assigned to them, even though no type annotation was used.

Type inference is useful for situations where you don't need to explicitly define types but still want TypeScript to perform type checking.

2. Interfaces and Types

In TypeScript, **interfaces** and **types** are two ways to define custom types. They allow you to specify the shape of an object, defining what properties it should have and what types those properties should be.

Interfaces

An **interface** is a way to define the shape of an object, including the types of its properties. Interfaces are flexible and are often used to define object structures.

```typescript
interface Person {
    name: string;
    age: number;
}

const person: Person = {
    name: "John",
    age: 30
};
```

In this example, we define a `Person` interface that expects an object with `name` and `age` properties, where `name` is a string and `age` is a number.

Interfaces can also define methods within them:

typescript

```
interface Animal {
    name: string;
    sound(): void; // Method declaration
}

const dog: Animal = {
    name: "Dog",
    sound: () => console.log("Woof!")
};

dog.sound(); // Outputs: Woof!
```

Types

A **type alias** is similar to an interface but more flexible. It can define a wide range of types, including primitive types, union types, and function types.

typescript

```
type Address = {
    street: string;
```

```
    city: string;
    zipCode: number;
};


const myAddress: Address = {
    street: "123 Main St",
    city: "New York",
    zipCode: 10001
};
```

While interfaces are typically used for objects, **type aliases** can be used for more complex type definitions, including unions or intersections:

typescript

```
type ID = string | number; // ID can be either a
string or a number
let userId: ID = 123; // Valid
userId = "abc"; // Also valid
```

3. Classes and Inheritance in TypeScript

TypeScript builds on JavaScript's class syntax and extends it with features such as type annotations and access modifiers. This allows you to write **object-oriented** code with better type safety and organization.

Defining Classes

A **class** in TypeScript is defined in a similar way to JavaScript, but with optional type annotations for properties and methods.

```typescript
class Car {
    make: string;
    model: string;
    year: number;

    constructor(make: string, model: string, year: number) {
        this.make = make;
        this.model = model;
        this.year = year;
    }

    getCarInfo(): string {
        return `${this.year} ${this.make} ${this.model}`;
    }
}

const myCar = new Car("Toyota", "Corolla", 2020);
console.log(myCar.getCarInfo()); // Outputs: 2020 Toyota Corolla
```

In this example:

- We define the `Car` class with three properties: `make`, `model`, and `year`.
- The constructor is used to initialize the values of these properties.
- The `getCarInfo` method returns a string containing the car's details.

Inheritance in TypeScript

TypeScript supports **inheritance**, allowing one class to inherit properties and methods from another class. This helps to reuse code and build more specific types based on general ones.

typescript

```
class ElectricCar extends Car {
    batteryLife: number;

    constructor(make: string, model: string, year:
number, batteryLife: number) {
        super(make, model, year); // Call the parent
class constructor
        this.batteryLife = batteryLife;
    }

    getCarInfo(): string {
```

```
        return `${super.getCarInfo()} with a battery
life of ${this.batteryLife} hours`;
    }
}


const myElectricCar = new ElectricCar("Tesla", "Model
S", 2021, 24);
console.log(myElectricCar.getCarInfo()); // Outputs:
2021 Tesla Model S with a battery life of 24 hours
```

In this example:

- `ElectricCar` extends `Car`, inheriting its properties and methods.
- We use the `super()` function to call the parent class's constructor, and then add a new property (`batteryLife`).
- The `getCarInfo` method is overridden to include information about the battery life.

4. Integrating TypeScript into JavaScript Projects

Integrating TypeScript into an existing JavaScript project is straightforward. TypeScript can coexist with JavaScript, meaning you can gradually adopt TypeScript features as needed.

Setting Up TypeScript in a Project

1. **Install TypeScript**: First, you need to install TypeScript in your project. If you are using npm, run:

    ```bash
    bash
    ```

    ```bash
    npm install typescript --save-dev
    ```

2. **Create a `tsconfig.json` File**: This file tells TypeScript how to compile your code. You can create it manually or by running:

    ```bash
    bash
    ```

    ```bash
    npx tsc --init
    ```

3. **Converting JavaScript to TypeScript**: Rename your `.js` files to `.ts` files. TypeScript will then analyze your code for any errors or missing type annotations.

4. **Gradual Adoption**: You don't need to convert the entire project to TypeScript at once. You can start by adding type annotations to a few files, and TypeScript will help identify potential issues.

Using TypeScript with Node.js

If you are working with Node.js, you can integrate TypeScript by installing the necessary packages:

bash

```bash
npm install typescript @types/node --save-dev
```

Then, you can write your server-side code in TypeScript and compile it using the TypeScript compiler (`tsc`).

typescript

```typescript
// server.ts
import { createServer } from "http";

const server = createServer((req, res) => {
    res.write("Hello, World!");
    res.end();
});

server.listen(3000, () => {
    console.log("Server running on port 3000");
});
```

You can then compile the TypeScript file using:

```bash
bash

npx tsc server.ts
```

This will generate a `server.js` file that can be run using Node.js.

Using TypeScript in the Browser

For browser-based applications, you can use TypeScript directly with modern build tools like **Webpack** or **Parcel** to compile TypeScript files into JavaScript

Hands-On Project: Convert an Existing JavaScript Project into TypeScript

In this project, we will take a simple JavaScript app and convert it to TypeScript, focusing on adding types and interfaces.

Step 1: JavaScript Version of the App

Here's a basic app that manages a list of tasks:

```javascript
javascript

let tasks = [];

function addTask(task) {
    tasks.push(task);
}
```

```
function listTasks() {
    tasks.forEach(task => console.log(task));
}


addTask("Buy groceries");
addTask("Clean the house");


listTasks();
```

Step 2: Converting to TypeScript

Now, we'll convert this code to TypeScript, adding types and an interface for the task.

```typescript
interface Task {
    id: number;
    description: string;
}

let tasks: Task[] = [];

function addTask(task: Task): void {
    tasks.push(task);
}

function listTasks(): void {
```

```
    tasks.forEach((task) => console.log(`${task.id}:
${task.description}`));
}


addTask({ id: 1, description: "Buy groceries" });
addTask({ id: 2, description: "Clean the house" });


listTasks();
```

Step 3: Explanation

1. **Task Interface**: We define an interface `Task` to specify the structure of each task object. Each task must have an `id` (a number) and a `description` (a string).
2. **Adding Types**: We specify that `tasks` is an array of `Task` objects (`Task[]`), and the functions `addTask` and `listTasks` are also typed.
3. **Adding a Task**: We create a task object that follows the `Task` interface and pass it to the `addTask` function.

This process of converting a JavaScript app to TypeScript involves adding types and ensuring that the code adheres to the structure defined by the interfaces and type annotations.

Conclusion

In this chapter, we've covered the core features of **TypeScript**, including type annotations, type inference, interfaces, classes, and inheritance. You've learned how TypeScript can enhance JavaScript development by catching errors early and providing better tooling and code organization.

By converting a JavaScript project into TypeScript, we demonstrated how TypeScript can improve the development process by making the code more maintainable and less error-prone. The use of **type annotations** and **interfaces** helps ensure that your application is built with the right structure, leading to fewer bugs and more predictable behavior.

As you continue to work with TypeScript, you'll be able to take advantage of its powerful static typing features, creating more robust, scalable, and maintainable applications.

Chapter 11: JavaScript Frameworks Overview

Overview

JavaScript frameworks have become a critical part of web development. They provide developers with powerful tools to build modern, dynamic, and responsive web applications. Frameworks help streamline the development process, reduce repetitive tasks, and improve code maintainability. Frameworks like **React**, **Angular**, and **Vue** have emerged as the leading choices for building web apps, each offering unique features and benefits.

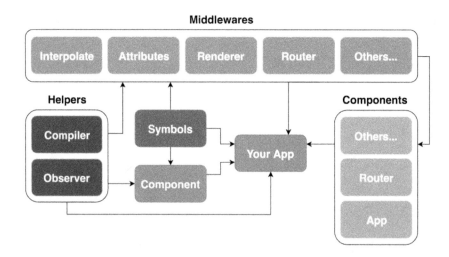

In this chapter, we will explore the core concepts of these three popular frameworks and see how they simplify development compared to using **vanilla JavaScript**. We will also build a simple weather app using **React** to demonstrate how one of these frameworks can be used in practice.

By the end of this chapter, you'll have a deeper understanding of when and why you might choose to use a framework over vanilla JavaScript and be familiar with key concepts such as **state management** and **component-based architecture**.

What is a JavaScript Framework?

A **JavaScript framework** is a pre-built set of libraries, tools, and conventions that help developers create web applications more efficiently. It typically includes reusable components, built-in tools for handling common tasks like routing, state management, and form validation, and often provides a structured way of organizing your code.

Unlike **vanilla JavaScript**, which provides no structure or built-in solutions for larger applications, a JavaScript framework provides an organized approach to developing web apps, often with features like:

- **Component-based architecture**: Organizing code into reusable pieces.

- **State management**: Handling changes to data in a predictable way.
- **Routing**: Managing navigation between different parts of the app.

While **vanilla JavaScript** gives developers more flexibility, frameworks come with trade-offs like **convention over configuration**—meaning they impose a certain structure but also make it easier to build large applications.

Overview of Popular JavaScript Frameworks

There are three major JavaScript frameworks that dominate the ecosystem: **React**, **Angular**, and **Vue**. Let's break down each framework, its key features, and when you might want to use them.

1. React

React is a **library** for building user interfaces, developed by Facebook. While it's often referred to as a framework, React focuses mainly on the **view layer** of an application, leaving other concerns such as routing and state management to other libraries. React is extremely popular for its simplicity, performance, and flexibility.

Key Concepts in React

- **Component-based architecture**: In React, the UI is broken down into components, which are small, reusable pieces of code that represent parts of the user interface. Components can be nested and managed hierarchically, which makes it easy to build large applications.

- **State management**: React introduces the concept of **state**, which is data that can change over time and affect how the component is rendered. Managing state in React is central to building interactive and dynamic applications.

- **JSX**: React uses **JSX**, a syntax extension that allows developers to write HTML-like code in their JavaScript. This makes it easier to define UI structures and embed JavaScript logic directly into the markup.

- **Virtual DOM**: React uses a virtual DOM to improve performance. The virtual DOM is an in-memory representation of the real DOM. When changes occur, React updates the virtual DOM and compares it to the real DOM to efficiently make updates.

When to Use React

- **Single-page applications (SPAs)**: React is particularly well-suited for building SPAs, where the entire app loads once, and only the parts of the page that need updating are re-rendered.

- **Complex UIs**: If your app has a complex user interface that involves lots of interactive elements, React's component-based architecture and state management make it a good choice.

2. Angular

Angular is a full-fledged **framework** developed by Google. Unlike React, which focuses only on the view layer, Angular is a complete solution for building large, enterprise-level applications. Angular provides everything you need out of the box, including routing, state management, and form handling.

Key Concepts in Angular

- **Component-based architecture**: Like React, Angular uses components to structure the UI. However, Angular components are more feature-rich and include things like lifecycle hooks and more advanced data binding.
- **Two-way data binding**: One of Angular's standout features is **two-way data binding**, which allows changes in the UI to automatically update the model (data), and changes in the model to automatically reflect in the UI. This makes it easier to work with forms and dynamic data.

- **Directives**: Directives are custom HTML attributes or elements that extend HTML's capabilities. Angular has built-in directives like `ngFor` and `ngIf`, but developers can also create their own.

- **RxJS**: Angular uses **RxJS** for handling asynchronous events and streams of data. RxJS provides powerful operators for working with observables, which makes it easier to handle complex data flows in your application.

When to Use Angular

- **Enterprise applications**: Angular is well-suited for building large-scale, complex applications due to its complete toolset and extensive documentation.

- **Comprehensive solutions**: If you need a full framework with built-in tools for routing, state management, and form handling, Angular is a good choice.

3. Vue

Vue is a progressive framework created by Evan You. It's often described as a **lightweight alternative** to Angular and React, offering a simple and flexible way to build interactive user interfaces. Vue is designed to be incrementally adoptable, which means you can use as much or as little of it as needed.

Key Concepts in Vue

- **Component-based architecture**: Like React and Angular, Vue uses components to manage UI elements. Vue's component system is lightweight and flexible, making it easier to get started with and use in existing projects.
- **Directives**: Vue uses **directives** such as `v-if`, `v-for`, and `v-bind` to handle data binding and control the behavior of the DOM.
- **Vuex**: Vue has a built-in state management library called **Vuex**, which is used to manage the application state across components.
- **Reactivity**: Vue automatically tracks dependencies and updates the view when data changes. This makes it easier to build dynamic UIs with less code.

When to Use Vue

- **Small to medium-sized projects**: Vue is a great choice for building small to medium-sized apps, or for integrating into existing projects. Its flexibility and simplicity make it ideal for projects where you don't need the full power of Angular or React.
- **Incrementally adoptable**: Vue allows you to progressively add it to existing projects, making it perfect for legacy

systems or when you want to gradually migrate to a modern framework.

When to Use a Framework vs. Vanilla JavaScript

While frameworks like React, Angular, and Vue offer significant advantages, there are times when it's better to use **vanilla JavaScript** (plain JavaScript without any framework). Here are some scenarios to consider:

Use a Framework When:

- **You're building a large-scale application**: Frameworks like Angular and React provide tools that simplify the development of complex, feature-rich applications.
- **You need a structured approach**: Frameworks enforce best practices, which makes them suitable for team-based projects or when working on large codebases.
- **You want performance optimization**: Frameworks like React (with its virtual DOM) and Vue's reactivity system optimize performance by minimizing DOM updates.
- **You need out-of-the-box features**: Frameworks often provide built-in solutions for routing, state management, and other common tasks, which saves you time and effort.

<u>Use Vanilla JavaScript When:</u>

- **Your project is small or simple**: For smaller applications or static websites, using a framework may add unnecessary complexity. Vanilla JavaScript may be sufficient.

- **You want complete control**: Vanilla JavaScript gives you complete flexibility and control over the application without the constraints of a framework.

- **You need a lightweight solution**: Frameworks can add additional overhead, which might be unnecessary for simple projects. Using vanilla JavaScript keeps the size of the project smaller.

Key Concepts in Each Framework

In this section, we'll explore the core concepts of **state management** and **component-based architecture**, which are crucial for understanding how these frameworks work.

<u>State Management</u>

State management refers to how an application manages and stores data that can change over time. In modern JavaScript frameworks, state is usually stored in components and is updated when necessary.

- **React** uses **state** within components to manage data and update the UI. React's unidirectional data flow makes it easy to manage state in a predictable way.
- **Angular** provides **two-way data binding**, meaning that changes to the state are automatically reflected in the UI and vice versa. Angular's state management is more integrated into the framework.
- **Vue** uses **Vuex** for state management, which helps manage state across multiple components in a centralized store.

Component-Based Architecture

Component-based architecture is the idea of breaking down a user interface into smaller, reusable pieces called components. Each component manages its own data and UI and can be composed with other components to build the application.

- **React**: Components in React are written as JavaScript functions or classes, and each component has its own state and lifecycle methods.
- **Angular**: Angular components are more feature-rich and can handle a wide range of tasks, including data binding, event handling, and more.
- **Vue**: Vue components are simple and flexible, making them easy to use and integrate into projects. Vue's reactive system makes it easy to update the UI when state changes.

Hands-On Project: Build a Weather App Using React

In this project, we'll build a simple **weather app** using **React**. The app will fetch weather data from a public API and display it on the page.

Step 1: Set Up the React Environment

To start, set up a basic React project using **Create React App,** a tool for setting up a new React project quickly.

bash

```
npx create-react-app weather-app
cd weather-app
npm start
```

This will create a new React project and start a development server at http://localhost:3000.

Step 2: Install Axios for API Requests

We will use **Axios** to fetch weather data from a public API. Install Axios by running:

bash

```
npm install axios
```

Step 3: Fetch Weather Data

In `App.js`, import **Axios** and write a function to fetch weather data from the **OpenWeatherMap API**.

```javascript
import React, { useState } from "react";
import axios from "axios";

function App() {
  const [weather, setWeather] = useState(null);
  const [city, setCity] = useState("");

  const fetchWeather = () => {
    const apiKey = "your-api-key-here";
    axios

.get(`https://api.openweathermap.org/data/2.5/weather?q=${city}&appid=${apiKey}&units=metric`)
      .then((response) => {
        setWeather(response.data);
      })
      .catch((error) => {
        console.error("Error fetching weather data:",
error);
      });
```

```
  };

  return (
    <div>
      <h1>Weather App</h1>
      <input
        type="text"
        placeholder="Enter city"
        value={city}
        onChange={(e) => setCity(e.target.value)}
      />
      <button onClick={fetchWeather}>Get
Weather</button>

      {weather && (
        <div>
          <h2>{weather.name}</h2>
          <p>Temperature: {weather.main.temp}°C</p>
          <p>Weather:
{weather.weather[0].description}</p>
          <p>Humidity: {weather.main.humidity}%</p>
        </div>
      )}
    </div>
  );
}

export default App;
```

<u>Step 4: Explanation</u>

1. **State Management**: We use React's `useState` hook to store the `city` input and the `weather` data.
2. **Fetching Data**: The `fetchWeather` function uses **Axios** to make a GET request to the OpenWeatherMap API and updates the `weather` state with the response data.
3. **Displaying Data**: When the data is fetched successfully, the weather information (city name, temperature, description, and humidity) is displayed dynamically on the page.

Conclusion

In this chapter, we explored popular JavaScript frameworks—**React**, **Angular**, and **Vue**—and discussed how they simplify development by providing tools and structure for building modern web applications. We also explored key concepts such as **state management**, **component-based architecture**, and how these frameworks handle complex user interfaces.

Through the **weather app project**, we demonstrated how to build a simple app with **React**, utilizing its component-based architecture and state management system to handle dynamic data. By understanding the core concepts of these frameworks, you will be better equipped to choose the right one for your project and build scalable, maintainable applications.

Chapter 12: Performance Optimization in JavaScript

Overview

JavaScript has come a long way, from being a small scripting language used for adding interactivity to web pages to becoming the backbone of large-scale web applications. As web applications grow in complexity, performance becomes increasingly important. Slow, inefficient JavaScript can lead to sluggish UIs, poor user experience, and increased load times, which can hurt both your application and user retention.

In this chapter, we will explore key techniques for **performance optimization** in JavaScript, focusing on how to improve performance in large applications. We'll cover **code splitting** and **lazy loading** to reduce initial load time, **tree-shaking** for eliminating unused code, **memory management** and **garbage collection** to optimize resource usage, and strategies to **optimize DOM rendering** to enhance responsiveness.

Finally, we'll work on a hands-on project where you will use browser developer tools to profile an application and identify performance bottlenecks. By the end of this chapter, you'll have a toolkit of performance optimization strategies that can be applied to your own projects.

Why JavaScript Performance Matters

Performance is critical in web development, especially when building modern web apps that rely on rich user interfaces and complex interactions. A sluggish application can lead to a poor user experience, increased bounce rates, and low engagement. For example, **performance issues** in JavaScript can manifest as:

- Slow page load times
- Laggy user interactions
- Delayed or jerky animations
- Excessive memory usage

Optimizing performance ensures your application runs smoothly, providing a fast and responsive experience to users. In this chapter, we will focus on practical techniques that can dramatically improve JavaScript performance.

1. Code Splitting and Lazy Loading

When building large JavaScript applications, loading all the JavaScript at once can result in long initial load times, especially if the application has many features or dependencies. **Code splitting** and **lazy loading** are powerful techniques to improve load times by only loading the necessary code when it's needed.

What is Code Splitting?

Code splitting involves breaking up your JavaScript into smaller pieces (or **chunks**) that can be loaded separately, rather than loading the entire JavaScript file at once. This reduces the amount of JavaScript that needs to be loaded initially, which speeds up page load times.

For example, a simple web app might only need certain features or libraries when the user navigates to specific pages. With code splitting, you can load only the necessary JavaScript for the page that the user is currently viewing.

Code Splitting Example (Webpack)

If you're using **Webpack**, you can configure code splitting with dynamic imports. This tells Webpack to create separate chunks for specific features.

```javascript
// Normal import
import { sum } from './math';

// Dynamic import with code splitting
```

```
const loadSquare = () =>
import('./square').then(module => module.default);
```

In the example above, `math.js` is statically imported, while `square.js` is dynamically imported when the function `loadSquare` is called. This helps reduce the amount of JavaScript loaded on initial page load.

What is Lazy Loading?

Lazy loading is the technique of loading code or resources only when they are needed. It is often used in conjunction with code splitting, where chunks of code are only loaded when the user interacts with a specific feature.

For example, images or components might not be loaded until they are visible on the screen.

```javascript
const button = document.getElementById('lazy-load-button');

button.addEventListener('click', () => {
    import('./heavyModule').then(module => {
        module.loadHeavyFeature();
    });
});
```

In this example, the heavy module is loaded only when the user clicks the button.

When to Use Code Splitting and Lazy Loading

- **Large applications**: For applications with many routes or features, code splitting can dramatically improve load times.
- **Interactive features**: If certain features of the app are rarely used, lazy loading can ensure those features are only loaded when needed.

2. Tree-Shaking for Unused Code Removal

Over time, JavaScript applications tend to accumulate unused code, particularly when third-party libraries or dependencies are used. **Tree-shaking** is a process that helps remove unused code from your final bundle, reducing its size and improving performance.

What is Tree-Shaking?

Tree-shaking is a feature in bundlers like **Webpack** that removes unused code from your JavaScript files during the bundling process. This is particularly useful when using libraries like **Lodash**, where only a subset of the available functions might be used.

Tree-Shaking Example

Consider a library that contains multiple utilities, but you only need a few functions:

```javascript
// lodash.js
import { map, filter } from 'lodash';

// Only `map` and `filter` will be included in the
final bundle.
```

In the example above, **tree-shaking** ensures that only the functions `map` and `filter` are included in the final bundle, while other unused functions from Lodash are removed.

How Does Tree-Shaking Work?

For tree-shaking to work, the code must be **ES6 module syntax** (i.e., `import`/`export`), as ES6 modules allow bundlers to statically analyze which parts of the code are used and which are not.

```javascript
// Example of ES6 imports
import { someFunction } from './utils';
```

This static analysis enables the bundler to exclude any functions that are not being imported or used in the final code.

When to Use Tree-Shaking

- **Libraries with many features**: If you're using a library with many functions but only need a few, tree-shaking helps reduce your bundle size.
- **Single-page applications (SPAs)**: For SPAs with lots of routes and features, tree-shaking can ensure that only the code necessary for the current page is included in the bundle.

3. Memory Management and Garbage Collection

Memory management is another critical aspect of performance optimization, especially for long-running JavaScript applications. JavaScript's **garbage collector** automatically manages memory by reclaiming space that is no longer used. However, developers must still be aware of how memory is used and ensure that unused objects are properly disposed of.

What is Garbage Collection?

Garbage collection is the process by which JavaScript automatically frees up memory that is no longer in use. It identifies objects that are no longer referenced and removes them from memory to prevent memory leaks.

For example:

javascript

```
let obj = { name: "John" };
obj = null; // The object is now eligible for garbage
collection
```

In this example, the object is no longer referenced by the `obj` variable, so it becomes eligible for garbage collection.

How to Manage Memory in JavaScript

While garbage collection is automatic, developers can take steps to minimize memory usage and avoid memory leaks:

- **Avoid global variables**: They can remain in memory for the entire lifetime of the application.
- **Use closures wisely**: Closures can hold references to variables and cause memory leaks if not managed properly.
- **Clean up event listeners**: When DOM elements are removed, make sure to remove any associated event listeners.

```javascript
// Avoid memory leaks
const button = document.getElementById('my-button');
button.addEventListener('click', () => {});

button.removeEventListener('click', () => {}); //
Clean up after use
```

When to Manage Memory Explicitly

- **Large-scale applications**: If your app runs for extended periods or has many complex interactions, you need to actively manage memory to avoid performance degradation.
- **Applications with frequent DOM updates**: Repeatedly adding and removing elements can lead to memory leaks if not handled correctly.

4. Optimizing Rendering in the DOM

One of the most noticeable performance bottlenecks in web applications is **rendering** in the **DOM**. Every time the state of the app changes, the DOM is updated, and this can be an expensive operation, especially for complex applications with many elements.

What Affects DOM Rendering?

The DOM is a tree structure that represents all the elements on a webpage. Every time an element changes, the browser has to update the DOM, which can lead to performance issues if not optimized.

- **Reflows**: A reflow occurs when the browser recalculates the layout of the page after a change. This can be an expensive operation, especially when it involves large portions of the DOM.
- **Repaints**: Repaints happen when visual changes occur but do not affect the layout (e.g., changing a color). While less expensive than reflows, they still contribute to performance issues.

Optimizing DOM Updates

- **Batch DOM updates**: Instead of updating the DOM multiple times, group DOM changes together to minimize reflows.

javascript

```
// Inefficient: Multiple reflows
document.body.style.width = "200px";
document.body.style.height = "200px";

// Efficient: Batching updates
```

```
document.body.style.cssText = 'width: 200px; height:
200px;';
```

- **Use `requestAnimationFrame` for animations**: For smooth animations, use `requestAnimationFrame` to schedule DOM updates before the next paint.

```
javascript
```

```
function animate() {
    // Update DOM elements here
    requestAnimationFrame(animate);
}
requestAnimationFrame(animate);
```

- **Avoid unnecessary DOM manipulations**: Manipulate the DOM only when necessary. Avoid excessive DOM traversal and manipulation, especially within loops.

When to Optimize DOM Rendering

- **Complex UIs**: If your app involves complex UIs with frequent updates (like an interactive dashboard or game), optimizing rendering will improve the user experience.
- **Mobile apps**: Mobile browsers are often less powerful than desktop browsers, so optimizing DOM updates is crucial for mobile web applications.

Hands-On Project: Profiling an App and Identifying Performance Bottlenecks

In this project, we'll take a sample web app and profile it using browser developer tools to identify performance bottlenecks. We'll use the Chrome DevTools to analyze the app's performance and make optimizations.

Step 1: Setting Up the Project

Start by creating a simple web app that has some performance bottlenecks. Here's a basic example:

```
html
```

```html
<!DOCTYPE html>
<html lang="en">
<head>
    <meta charset="UTF-8">
    <meta name="viewport" content="width=device-width, initial-scale=1.0">
    <title>Performance Test</title>
</head>
<body>
    <h1>Performance Bottleneck Demo</h1>
    <button id="startButton">Start Process</button>
    <script src="app.js"></script>
</body>
</html>
```

```javascript
// app.js
document.getElementById("startButton").addEventListen
er("click", function() {
    let start = Date.now();
    let sum = 0;
    for (let i = 0; i < 10000000; i++) {
        sum += i;
    }
    console.log("Calculation took: " + (Date.now() -
start) + " ms");
});
```

This simple app runs a computationally expensive operation when the button is clicked.

Step 2: Profiling the App with Chrome DevTools

1. Open the app in **Google Chrome**.
2. Right-click on the page and select **Inspect** to open **DevTools**.
3. Go to the **Performance** tab and click **Record**.
4. Click the **Start Process** button on the app.
5. Stop the recording after the process completes.

DevTools will show a detailed breakdown of where the most time was spent. In this case, you'll notice that the loop is taking up a lot of CPU time.

Step 3: Optimizing the App

Now, let's optimize the app by breaking the long-running task into smaller chunks using **setTimeout** to avoid blocking the main thread.

```javascript
document.getElementById("startButton").addEventListener("click", function() {
    let start = Date.now();
    let sum = 0;
    let i = 0;

    function calculate() {
        if (i < 10000000) {
            sum += i;
            i++;
            requestAnimationFrame(calculate);
        } else {
            console.log("Calculation took: " + (Date.now() - start) + " ms");
        }
    }

    calculate();
});
```

This modification ensures that the long-running task is broken into smaller chunks, and the browser remains responsive during the calculation.

Conclusion

In this chapter, we explored several key techniques for optimizing JavaScript performance, especially in large applications. We covered **code splitting** and **lazy loading** to reduce initial load times, **tree-shaking** to remove unused code, **memory management** to optimize resource usage, and **optimizing DOM rendering** to improve responsiveness. We also went through a hands-on project where you used **Chrome DevTools** to profile and optimize a simple app.

By applying these performance optimization techniques, you can ensure that your JavaScript applications are fast, responsive, and scalable. As web applications grow in complexity, performance optimization becomes a crucial aspect of maintaining a great user experience. With the tools and techniques covered in this chapter, you are now equipped to tackle performance bottlenecks and optimize your JavaScript code for better performance.

Chapter 13: Testing and Debugging JavaScript

Overview

Testing and debugging are critical aspects of the software development process, especially when it comes to JavaScript applications. As JavaScript has become the backbone of web development, ensuring your code is reliable, maintainable, and bug-free is more important than ever.

In this chapter, we'll explore the essential aspects of testing JavaScript, including **unit testing, debugging tools**, and **test-driven development (TDD)**. You'll learn how to use modern testing frameworks like **Jest** and **Mocha** to test your functions and components. We'll also dive into the most commonly used debugging tools in modern browsers, and how to write effective **test cases**.

The chapter will conclude with a hands-on project, where you'll write **unit tests** for a JavaScript application and run them using **Jest**. By the end of this chapter, you'll have a solid understanding of testing and debugging practices that will improve the quality and reliability of your JavaScript code.

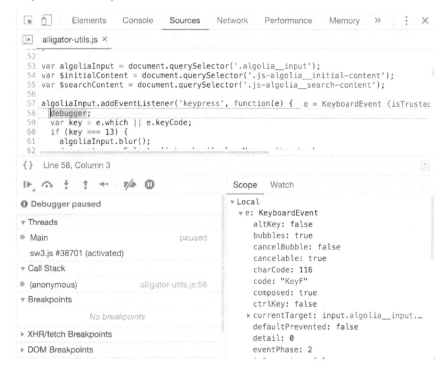

The Importance of Testing in JavaScript

Testing is a fundamental practice in software development that helps ensure the correctness of your code, especially as applications grow in complexity. Testing provides several key benefits:

1. **Early Detection of Bugs**: Running tests regularly helps identify problems early, preventing bugs from affecting users.

2. **Code Confidence**: When tests are in place, developers can make changes with confidence, knowing that the tests will catch regressions.

3. **Documentation**: Well-written tests serve as documentation for your code, providing insights into how different parts of the system interact and what their expected behavior is.

4. **Improved Code Quality**: Writing tests forces developers to think critically about their code and its behavior, leading to cleaner and more maintainable code.

In JavaScript, testing is especially important because the language is often used in environments with high user interaction, like browsers. A bug in a user-facing app can have a significant impact on the user experience. That's why **unit testing** (testing individual functions) and **debugging** (finding and fixing errors in code) are crucial skills for JavaScript developers.

Unit Testing with Jest or Mocha

Unit testing involves testing individual pieces of your code, usually functions, to ensure they behave as expected. This process typically involves writing **test cases**, which define what your code should do under various conditions.

Why Use a Testing Framework?

A **testing framework** provides tools for writing, organizing, and running tests. Popular JavaScript testing frameworks like **Jest** and **Mocha** make the process of testing more efficient and streamlined. They provide helpful assertions, tools for mocking data, and a structured approach for organizing test files.

1. Jest

Jest is a JavaScript testing framework developed by Facebook, and it's widely used for testing React applications. It's simple to set up and comes with everything you need to write tests, including an assertion library, mocks, and a test runner.

Jest is particularly useful because:

- It provides a simple syntax for writing tests.
- It automatically runs all tests and gives detailed output.
- Jest comes with built-in support for mocking and spying on functions.

Basic Jest Test

Here's an example of how to write a simple Jest test for a function:

```
javascript
```

```
// sum.js
function sum(a, b) {
  return a + b;
}

module.exports = sum;

// sum.test.js
const sum = require('./sum');

test('adds 1 + 2 to equal 3', () => {
  expect(sum(1, 2)).toBe(3);
});
```

- The `test()` function defines a test case, with the first argument being a description of the test and the second being a callback function containing the test logic.
- `expect()` is used to make assertions about the result of the code being tested. In this case, we're checking that `sum(1, 2)` returns 3.
- `toBe()` is a matcher that checks whether the value returned by the function matches the expected value.

To run the tests, simply run the command:

```bash
```

```
npm test
```

Jest will automatically find all the tests in your project and execute them.

Mocha is another popular JavaScript testing framework. Unlike Jest, Mocha is more flexible, and you can pair it with other libraries like **Chai** for assertions and **Sinon** for spies, mocks, and stubs.

Mocha is great for:

- Its flexibility in integrating with other libraries.
- Supporting both **unit testing** and **integration testing**.
- Providing useful reporting features for large test suites.

Basic Mocha Test

Here's an example of how you would write a test using **Mocha** and **Chai**:

javascript

```
// sum.js
function sum(a, b) {
  return a + b;
}

module.exports = sum;
```

```
// test.js
const chai = require('chai');
const sum = require('./sum');
const expect = chai.expect;

describe('sum function', function() {
  it('should add 1 + 2 to equal 3', function() {
    expect(sum(1, 2)).to.equal(3);
  });
});
```

In this example:

- `describe()` is used to group related tests together.
- `it()` defines an individual test case.
- `expect()` is an assertion library that provides easy-to-read syntax for testing.

To run the tests, you would use a test runner like **Mocha** in combination with a test command:

```bash
bash
```

```
mocha test.js
```

Writing Test Cases for Functions and Components

The core of unit testing is writing **test cases** that validate the behavior of individual units of your code. In this section, we'll look at how to write tests for both **functions** and **components**.

1. Writing Test Cases for Functions

A **function** is a self-contained block of code designed to perform a specific task. Testing functions involves checking if the input to the function produces the expected output.

Example: Testing a Function

Let's say we have a function that calculates the area of a rectangle:

javascript

```javascript
function calculateArea(length, width) {
  return length * width;
}
```

We can write a test case to ensure it behaves as expected:

javascript

```
test('calculateArea should return the correct area',
() => {
  expect(calculateArea(5, 10)).toBe(50);
});
```

This test checks if the `calculateArea` function correctly calculates the area for a rectangle with a length of 5 and a width of 10.

2. Writing Test Cases for Components (React)

In modern web development, you often work with **UI components**. Testing components ensures that the UI renders correctly based on different states and interactions.

Example: Testing a React Component

Let's say we have a simple React component that displays the area of a rectangle:

```javascript
import React from 'react';

function AreaComponent({ length, width }) {
  return (
    <div>
      The area is: {length * width}
```

```
      </div>
   );
}


export default AreaComponent;
```

To test this component, we use **React Testing Library** in combination with **Jest**:

javascript

```javascript
import { render, screen } from '@testing-library/react';
import AreaComponent from './AreaComponent';

test('displays the correct area', () => {
   render(<AreaComponent length={5} width={10} />);
   const areaText = screen.getByText(/The area is:/);
   expect(areaText).toHaveTextContent('The area is: 50');
});
```

This test renders the `AreaComponent` with the provided `length` and `width` props and checks if the correct area is displayed in the component.

Debugging Tools in Modern Browsers

Debugging is an essential part of the development process. Modern browsers come equipped with powerful **developer tools** that allow you to inspect and debug JavaScript code.

1. Using Chrome DevTools

Chrome DevTools is a suite of web authoring and debugging tools built into Google Chrome. Here are some key features you can use:

- **Console**: View logs, errors, and warnings in your code. You can also use `console.log()` to log values and inspect variables.
- **Sources Panel**: Set breakpoints in your JavaScript code to pause execution and step through it line by line.
- **Network Panel**: Monitor network requests, including API calls, and inspect their responses.
- **Performance Panel**: Profile the performance of your app, including JavaScript execution and rendering performance.
- **Elements Panel**: Inspect and modify the DOM in real-time.

2. Using the Debugger Statement

You can also use the `debugger` statement to pause code execution at specific points and inspect the call stack.

```javascript
function sum(a, b) {
  debugger; // Pauses execution here
  return a + b;
}
```

When the `debugger` statement is encountered, the browser's developer tools will open, and you can inspect the current state of your application.

Test-Driven Development (TDD)

Test-Driven Development (TDD) is a development process where you write tests before writing the actual code. The TDD process follows these steps:

1. **Write a failing test**: Start by writing a test that describes the behavior you want to implement. Since the functionality isn't written yet, the test will fail.
2. **Write the code**: Write the minimum amount of code necessary to make the test pass.
3. **Refactor**: Clean up the code, ensuring that it's still passing the test.

Example of TDD Process

Let's say we need to write a function that calculates the sum of an array of numbers. We would start by writing a test:

javascript

```
test('sumArray should return the correct sum', () =>
{
  expect(sumArray([1, 2, 3])).toBe(6);
});
```

Since the `sumArray` function doesn't exist yet, the test will fail. Now, we write the minimal code to make the test pass:

javascript

```
function sumArray(arr) {
  return arr.reduce((sum, num) => sum + num, 0);
}
```

Finally, we refactor the code to make it cleaner while ensuring the test still passes.

Hands-On Project: Write Unit Tests for a JavaScript App Using Jest

In this project, we'll write unit tests for a JavaScript app that calculates the total price of items in a shopping cart.

Step 1: Create the JavaScript App

javascript

```javascript
// cart.js
function calculateTotal(cart) {
  return cart.reduce((total, item) => total +
item.price, 0);
}

function addItem(cart, item) {
  cart.push(item);
  return cart;
}

module.exports = { calculateTotal, addItem };
```

Step 2: Write Unit Tests Using Jest

Now, let's write unit tests for the `calculateTotal` and `addItem` functions.

javascript

```javascript
// cart.test.js
const { calculateTotal, addItem } =
require('./cart');

test('calculateTotal should return correct total', ()
=> {
  const cart = [{ price: 20 }, { price: 30 }];
```

```
  expect(calculateTotal(cart)).toBe(50);
});

test('addItem should add item to the cart', () => {
  const cart = [{ price: 20 }];
  const newItem = { price: 30 };
  const updatedCart = addItem(cart, newItem);
  expect(updatedCart.length).toBe(2);
  expect(updatedCart[1].price).toBe(30);
});
```

Step 3: Run the Tests

To run the tests, simply run:

```bash
bash
```

```
npm test
```

Jest will run the tests and display the results, helping you identify any failing tests or errors.

Conclusion

In this chapter, we explored the crucial aspects of **testing** and **debugging** in JavaScript development. We covered the importance of testing, the various tools and strategies for writing unit tests with **Jest** and **Mocha,** and debugging tools in modern browsers. We also introduced **Test-Driven Development (TDD)**, which encourages writing tests before writing the actual code, helping to ensure better software quality.

Through the **hands-on project**, you wrote unit tests for a shopping cart application using Jest and learned how to test functions effectively. By applying the concepts in this chapter, you'll be able to write more reliable and maintainable JavaScript code, reduce bugs, and improve the overall quality of your applications.

Testing and debugging are essential skills for every JavaScript developer. With these techniques, you can build more robust, user-friendly applications and ensure your code behaves as expected in different scenarios.

Chapter 14: JavaScript in Modern Web Applications

Overview

JavaScript is the backbone of modern web development. It powers interactive user interfaces, dynamic content, and sophisticated client-server interactions. With the rise of **single-page applications (SPAs)**, JavaScript frameworks like **React** and **Vue**, and modern deployment tools like **Netlify** and **Vercel**, developers can now build full-fledged, feature-rich web applications that perform seamlessly across devices and browsers.

In this chapter, we will explore how JavaScript is used to create **modern web applications** using the latest tools and techniques. You will learn how to build **single-page applications (SPAs)**, implement **routing** and **state management**, and deploy your applications to production. We'll also walk through a hands-on project to build and deploy a **full-stack app** that includes **authentication** and **data persistence**.

By the end of this chapter, you'll be equipped with the knowledge to create, manage, and deploy sophisticated web applications that are production-ready and performant.

1. Single-Page Applications (SPAs)

In traditional multi-page web applications, each time a user interacts with the app, the browser loads a new page from the server. This process can be slow and result in a poor user experience due to constant reloading. **Single-page applications (SPAs)** offer a solution by loading a single HTML page and dynamically updating the content as needed, without refreshing the entire page.

What is a Single-Page Application (SPA)?

An SPA is a type of web application where the content on the page is updated dynamically using JavaScript, rather than reloading entire pages. This results in a smoother, faster, and more interactive user experience. SPAs interact with the server asynchronously (using **AJAX** or **fetch**), allowing users to navigate between different views without reloading the page.

Advantages of SPAs

- **Faster performance**: SPAs only load necessary data and update the view dynamically, which makes them faster than traditional multi-page apps.

- **Smooth user experience**: Since the page doesn't reload with every action, the user experience is more fluid, and interactions feel quicker.
- **Simplified routing**: SPAs manage routing within the app, allowing users to navigate between views without server-side page reloads.

SPA Example

Consider a simple blog app. In a traditional multi-page application, each time the user navigates between blog posts, a new page is loaded from the server. In an SPA, only the necessary content is updated, making the navigation seamless and faster.

javascript

```javascript
// JavaScript for an SPA route
function loadPost(postId) {
  fetch(`/api/posts/${postId}`)
    .then(response => response.json())
    .then(post => {
      document.getElementById('content').innerHTML =
post.content;
    });
}
```

In this example, clicking on a blog post link loads the content without refreshing the page, updating the DOM dynamically.

2. Using Frameworks like React or Vue for Building Modern Web Apps

Frameworks like **React** and **Vue** are essential tools for building modern SPAs. These frameworks help manage the complexity of building interactive UIs by providing structured approaches to organizing your code and handling the state and UI updates.

React

React is a **JavaScript library** for building user interfaces, primarily used for building SPAs. It's component-based, meaning that you break your UI into small, reusable components that manage their own state and render data. React uses a **virtual DOM** to optimize updates and improve performance.

Key Features of React

- **Component-based architecture**: React breaks down the UI into independent components, each responsible for rendering a part of the UI.
- **JSX**: React uses **JSX**, which allows you to write HTML-like code in JavaScript. This makes it easier to define and work with UI components.
- **State management**: React allows you to manage state within components using the `useState` hook (or the `setState` method in class components).

React Example

Here's a simple React component that displays a list of items:

javascript

```javascript
import React, { useState } from 'react';

function ItemList() {
  const [items, setItems] = useState(['Item 1', 'Item
2', 'Item 3']);

  return (
    <div>
      <h2>Item List</h2>
      <ul>
        {items.map(item => (
          <li key={item}>{item}</li>
        ))}
      </ul>
    </div>
  );
}

export default ItemList;
```

In this example:

- The `ItemList` component uses the `useState` hook to manage the list of items.
- The `map()` function is used to iterate over the items and display them in an unordered list.

React's declarative approach allows developers to focus on defining the UI in terms of state, and React handles updating the DOM efficiently.

Vue

Vue.js is another powerful **JavaScript framework** for building UIs, often seen as a more flexible and lightweight alternative to React. Vue's **reactivity system** allows data to automatically update the DOM when it changes, making it ideal for building dynamic web applications.

Key Features of Vue

- **Component-based**: Like React, Vue is component-based, allowing you to break your app into small, reusable components.
- **Directives**: Vue provides custom HTML attributes called **directives** (e.g., `v-if`, `v-for`) to handle DOM manipulations declaratively.

- **Vuex for state management**: Vue uses **Vuex** as its state management solution to manage state across multiple components.

Vue Example

Here's how you might create a simple Vue component to display a list of items:

```javascript
<template>
  <div>
    <h2>Item List</h2>
    <ul>
      <li v-for="item in items" :key="item">{{ item }}</li>
    </ul>
  </div>
</template>

<script>
export default {
  data() {
    return {
      items: ['Item 1', 'Item 2', 'Item 3']
    };
  }
};
```

```
</script>
```

In this example:

- The `v-for` directive is used to loop through the `items` array and render each item in the list.
- The `data()` function is used to define the component's state.

Vue's declarative syntax and reactivity system make it simple to work with dynamic content.

3. Routing and State Management

Routing in SPAs

Routing is the process of changing views or pages within a single-page application without reloading the entire page. In SPAs, **client-side routing** is used to manage navigation, and frameworks like React and Vue provide built-in tools to handle it.

React Router

In React, **React Router** is the most popular solution for routing. It allows you to define different routes and render different components based on the URL.

```javascript
import React from 'react';
import { BrowserRouter as Router, Route, Switch }
from 'react-router-dom';

function App() {
  return (
    <Router>
      <Switch>
        <Route path="/" exact component={HomePage} />
        <Route path="/about" component={AboutPage} />
      </Switch>
    </Router>
  );
}
```

This example uses `BrowserRouter` to handle routing, and the `Switch` component ensures only one route is rendered at a time. You can define routes for different pages of your app, such as the homepage and the about page.

Vue Router

In Vue, **Vue Router** is the official router for managing routes in a Vue app. Here's how you might set up routing:

```javascript
import Vue from 'vue';
import Router from 'vue-router';
import HomePage from './HomePage.vue';
import AboutPage from './AboutPage.vue';

Vue.use(Router);

const router = new Router({
  routes: [
    { path: '/', component: HomePage },
    { path: '/about', component: AboutPage }
  ]
});

export default router;
```

Vue Router works similarly to React Router, allowing you to map URL paths to components.

State Management

Managing application state can be complex, especially in large applications. Frameworks like React and Vue provide built-in tools or libraries for managing state across multiple components.

React: State and Context API

In React, you can manage local component state using the `useState` hook, but for more complex state management, you can use the **Context API** or external libraries like **Redux**.

```javascript
import React, { useContext } from 'react';

const UserContext = React.createContext();

function UserProfile() {
  const user = useContext(UserContext);
  return <div>Hello, {user.name}</div>;
}

function App() {
  const user = { name: 'John Doe' };

  return (
    <UserContext.Provider value={user}>
      <UserProfile />
    </UserContext.Provider>
  );
}
```

In this example, we use the `Context` API to pass down the `user` data across components.

Vuex for Vue

In Vue, **Vuex** is used for managing state across components in a centralized store. Here's a simple example of using Vuex:

```javascript
import Vue from 'vue';
import Vuex from 'vuex';

Vue.use(Vuex);

const store = new Vuex.Store({
  state: {
    user: { name: 'John Doe' }
  },
  getters: {
    userName: state => state.user.name
  }
});

new Vue({
  store,
  computed: {
    userName() {
      return this.$store.getters.userName;
    }
  }
});
```

In this example, the `user` data is stored in Vuex, and we can access it using getters.

4. Deploying JavaScript Apps to Production

Once your web app is ready, the next step is to deploy it to production. Tools like **Netlify** and **Vercel** make it easy to deploy JavaScript applications quickly and reliably.

Netlify

Netlify is a platform for deploying static websites and web apps. It integrates seamlessly with tools like React, Vue, and Gatsby.

- **Continuous deployment**: Netlify automatically deploys your app whenever you push changes to your Git repository (GitHub, GitLab, etc.).
- **Serverless functions**: You can add backend logic using **serverless functions** without needing a full server.

To deploy with Netlify:

1. Push your project to GitHub.
2. Connect your GitHub repo to Netlify.
3. Configure build settings (e.g., build command for React: `npm run build`).
4. Netlify will automatically deploy your app to a live URL.

Vercel

Vercel is another deployment platform, similar to Netlify, that focuses on serverless deployment. Vercel is ideal for deploying static sites and front-end frameworks like Next.js, React, and Vue.

- **Instant previews**: Vercel creates preview deployments for every pull request, allowing you to preview changes before they're merged.
- **Serverless functions**: Like Netlify, Vercel allows you to deploy serverless functions alongside your static app.

To deploy with Vercel:

1. Push your project to GitHub.
2. Connect your GitHub repo to Vercel.
3. Vercel automatically builds and deploys your app.

Hands-On Project: Build and Deploy a Full-Stack App Using a JavaScript Framework with Authentication and Data Persistence

In this hands-on project, we'll build a full-stack application using **React** for the front-end, **Node.js** for the back-end, and **MongoDB** for data persistence. The app will include **authentication** using **JWT (JSON Web Tokens)** and **data persistence** to store user data.

Step 1: Set Up the Backend with Node.js and Express

1. **Create a Node.js app** and install dependencies:

bash

```
mkdir my-fullstack-app
cd my-fullstack-app
npm init -y
npm install express mongoose jsonwebtoken bcryptjs
```

2. **Create a basic Express server:**

javascript

```
const express = require('express');
const app = express();
const mongoose = require('mongoose');

mongoose.connect('mongodb://localhost/mydb', {
useNewUrlParser: true, useUnifiedTopology: true });

app.listen(5000, () => {
  console.log('Server running on
http://localhost:5000');
});
```

3. **Set up routes for authentication** using JWT.

Step 2: Set Up the Frontend with React

1. **Create a React app:**

bash

```
npx create-react-app client
cd client
npm install axios react-router-dom
```

2. **Set up components for login, registration, and user dashboard.**
3. **Implement authentication** using JWT and React's **Context API**.

Step 3: Connect Frontend and Backend

1. **Send login requests** from the React app to the Node.js backend.
2. **Store the JWT** in **localStorage** for authentication.

Step 4: Deploy to Production

1. **Deploy the front-end** on **Netlify** or **Vercel**.
2. **Deploy the back-end** on **Heroku** or **DigitalOcean**.

Conclusion

In this chapter, we explored how to build sophisticated web applications using **JavaScript** frameworks like **React** and **Vue**. We covered key concepts such as **single-page applications (SPAs)**, **routing, state management**, and how to deploy JavaScript applications to production using tools like **Netlify** and **Vercel**.

Through the hands-on project, we learned how to build a **full-stack app** that incorporates **authentication, data persistence**, and **front-end and back-end integration**. By applying these techniques, you can create modern, scalable web applications that perform well and provide a seamless user experience.

With this knowledge, you're now ready to build, deploy, and maintain complex JavaScript applications with the latest tools and frameworks.

Chapter 15: Building Scalable Applications with Microservices

Overview

In modern software development, scalability is a crucial factor for applications that grow in size and complexity. One of the most effective ways to design scalable systems is through the **microservices architecture**. Microservices break down an application into smaller, self-contained services that communicate with each other, making it easier to scale and maintain each part of the application independently.

In this chapter, you will learn how to build scalable JavaScript applications using **microservices**. We will cover the fundamentals of **microservices architecture**, how to break down applications into smaller services, and how these services can communicate with each other. Additionally, we will explore how to **Dockerize** your microservices and deploy them efficiently.

By the end of this chapter, you will have a strong foundation in microservices architecture and be able to build and deploy a microservices-based system using **JavaScript**, **Node.js**, and **Docker**.

What is Microservices Architecture?

Microservices architecture is an approach to software development where a large application is broken down into smaller, independent services that each perform a specific task or business function. Each microservice is a self-contained unit, meaning it can be developed, deployed, and scaled independently of the others. Microservices typically communicate with each other over **network protocols** like **HTTP** or **message queues**.

Characteristics of Microservices Architecture

- **Independent Services**: Each microservice is an independent unit responsible for a single part of the application, such as user management, order processing, or inventory tracking.
- **Scalability**: Microservices allow individual services to scale independently, ensuring that resources are allocated efficiently.
- **Resilience**: If one microservice fails, it doesn't necessarily affect the entire application, as other services can continue to run.

- **Technology Agnostic**: Each microservice can be built with a different technology stack, depending on its requirements.

In contrast to traditional **monolithic architecture**, where all features and functionalities are tightly coupled and deployed together, microservices allow for more flexible development and easier scaling.

Breaking Down Applications into Smaller Services

Breaking down an application into microservices involves identifying the core functionalities of the application and separating them into distinct, self-contained services. Each microservice should have a well-defined responsibility and handle a specific business function.

Steps to Break Down an Application into Microservices

1. **Identify Core Domains**: Start by identifying the main business domains or functionalities within your application. For instance, if you're building an e-commerce app, the core domains could be **user management**, **product catalog**, **orders**, and **payment processing**.
2. **Define Microservices**: For each domain, define a microservice. Each microservice will focus on one specific business function and will have its own database, logic, and API.

Example:

- o **User Service**: Manages user registration, login, and profiles.
- o **Product Service**: Manages product information, catalog, and inventory.
- o **Order Service**: Handles order placement, status, and history.
- o **Payment Service**: Manages payment processing and transaction records.

3. **Define Boundaries and Interfaces**: Each microservice should have a clear boundary, meaning that it should not depend on other services for its core functionality. If microservices need to interact, they should do so via **well-defined APIs**.

4. **Data Ownership**: Each microservice should own its data. This prevents data duplication and makes it easier to scale and manage the data independently for each service.

Communication Between Microservices

Once we have multiple microservices, we need to define how they will communicate with each other. There are several methods for communication between microservices, including **REST APIs**, **GraphQL**, and **message queues**.

1. REST APIs

REST (Representational State Transfer) is the most common method for communication between microservices. Each microservice exposes an HTTP API that other services can call to access its data or trigger actions.

For instance, the **User Service** might expose a GET /users/{id} endpoint to retrieve user information, while the **Order Service** might call this API to associate a user with an order.

Example: REST API in Node.js
javascript

```javascript
const express = require('express');
const app = express();

// Simple user service with a GET endpoint
app.get('/users/:id', (req, res) => {
  const userId = req.params.id;
  // Fetch user data from database (simulated here)
  res.json({ id: userId, name: 'John Doe' });
});

app.listen(3000, () => {
  console.log('User Service is running on port
3000');
});
```

2. GraphQL

GraphQL is an alternative to REST that provides more flexibility by allowing clients to specify exactly what data they need from the service. It's particularly useful when you need to query multiple services at once or get complex data from multiple sources.

In GraphQL, each microservice can expose a **GraphQL endpoint**, and the client can request specific data fields.

3. Message Queues

For asynchronous communication, microservices often use **message queues** like **RabbitMQ**, **Kafka**, or **Amazon SQS**. A microservice can publish a message to a queue, and other microservices can listen to the queue and process the message.

Example: Using RabbitMQ in Node.js
```javascript
const amqp = require('amqplib/callback_api');

// Connect to RabbitMQ
amqp.connect('amqp://localhost', (error, connection)
=> {
  connection.createChannel((error, channel) => {
    const queue = 'orderQueue';
    const msg = 'Order received';
```

```
    channel.assertQueue(queue, { durable: false });
    channel.sendToQueue(queue, Buffer.from(msg));
    console.log("Sent: %s", msg);
  });
});
```

In this example, the **Order Service** sends a message to a queue that other services (e.g., **Payment Service**) can consume.

Dockerizing and Deploying Microservices

One of the key advantages of microservices is their ability to scale and run independently. **Docker** provides a simple and effective way to containerize each microservice, ensuring that they can run in isolated environments with all the necessary dependencies.

What is Docker?

Docker is a platform for developing, shipping, and running applications inside **containers**. Containers package an application and its dependencies together, ensuring that it runs consistently across different environments.

Dockerizing a Microservice

Each microservice can be containerized with Docker by writing a **Dockerfile** that defines how to build the container. Here's an example Dockerfile for the user service:

```
dockerfile

# Use the official Node.js image
FROM node:14

# Set the working directory
WORKDIR /usr/src/app

#  the application code into the container
 .  .

# Install dependencies
RUN npm install

# Expose the port the app runs on
EXPOSE 3000

# Start the app
CMD ["node", "app.js"]
```

This Dockerfile will create a container for the user service. You can then build and run the container using Docker commands:

```bash
bash

docker build -t user-service .
docker run -p 3000:3000 user-service
```

Setting Up Docker Compose

If you have multiple microservices, managing them with Docker Compose makes it easier to define and run multi-container Docker applications. Here's a basic `docker-compose.yml` file:

yaml

```
version: '3'
services:
  user-service:
    build: ./user-service
    ports:
      - "3000:3000"
  order-service:
    build: ./order-service
    ports:
      - "4000:4000"
```

This file will spin up both the **User Service** and **Order Service** in separate containers.

Deploying Microservices

Once your microservices are Dockerized, you can deploy them to a cloud provider like **AWS**, **Google Cloud**, or **Azure**, or use platforms like **Kubernetes** for managing containerized microservices at scale. Alternatively, platforms like **Heroku**, **Netlify**, or **Vercel** offer simple deployment options for microservices-based applications.

Hands-On Project: Create a Basic Microservices-Based System Using JavaScript, Node.js, and Docker

In this hands-on project, we'll create a basic microservices-based application using **JavaScript**, **Node.js**, and **Docker**. The app will have two services: **User Service** and **Order Service**, and they will communicate using **REST APIs**.

Step 1: Set Up the User Service

1. Create a directory for the **user-service** and initialize a Node.js project:

bash

```bash
mkdir user-service
cd user-service
npm init -y
npm install express
```

2. Create app.js for the user service:

javascript

```javascript
const express = require('express');
const app = express();

app.get('/users/:id', (req, res) => {
```

```
  const userId = req.params.id;
  res.json({ id: userId, name: 'John Doe' });
});
```

```
app.listen(3000, () => {
  console.log('User Service is running on port
3000');
});
```

3. Create a **Dockerfile** for the user service as shown earlier.

Step 2: Set Up the Order Service

1. Create a directory for the **order-service** and initialize a Node.js project:

bash

```
mkdir order-service
cd order-service
npm init -y
npm install express
```

2. Create app.js for the order service:

javascript

```
const express = require('express');
const app = express();
const axios = require('axios');
```

```
app.get('/orders/:id', async (req, res) => {
  const orderId = req.params.id;
  const userResponse = await axios.get(`http://user-
service:3000/users/${orderId}`);
  res.json({ orderId, user: userResponse.data });
});

app.listen(4000, () => {
  console.log('Order Service is running on port
4000');
});
```

3. Create a **Dockerfile** for the order service.

Step 3: Create Docker Compose File

In the root directory, create a `docker-compose.yml` file:

yaml

```
version: '3'
services:
  user-service:
    build: ./user-service
    ports:
      - "3000:3000"
  order-service:
    build: ./order-service
    ports:
```

```
      -  "4000:4000"
   depends_on:
      - user-service
```

Step 4: Run the Microservices

Run the microservices using Docker Compose:

```bash
bash
```

```
docker-compose up --build
```

This will spin up both the **User Service** and **Order Service** in separate containers. You can test the setup by navigating to `http://localhost:4000/orders/1`, and the order service will fetch user data from the user service.

Conclusion

In this chapter, we explored how to design and implement scalable applications using the **microservices architecture**. We covered key concepts such as breaking applications into smaller services, communication between microservices using **REST APIs**, and how to Dockerize and deploy microservices for production.

Through the **hands-on project**, we built a simple microservices-based system using **JavaScript**, **Node.js**, and **Docker**. By applying the concepts and techniques in this chapter, you now have the foundation to build scalable, maintainable, and independent services in your JavaScript applications.

As microservices become more widely used, understanding how to design, build, and deploy them will be an invaluable skill for developing modern, scalable web applications.